Everyday Wisdom
to
Satisfy Your Soul

Everyday
Wisdom
to
Satisfy
Your Soul

Pamela L. McQuade

BARBOUR
PUBLISHING

© 2003 by Barbour Publishing, Inc.

Written by Pamela L. McQuade

Print ISBN 978-1-64352-685-0

Published by Barbour Publishing, Inc., 1810 Barbour Drive, Uhrichsville, Ohio 44683, www.barbourbooks.com

Our mission is to inspire the world with the life-changing message of the Bible.

 Member of the Evangelical Christian Publishers Association

Printed in the United States of America.

"Store up for yourselves
treasures in heaven. . . .
For where your treasure is,
there your heart will be also."

Matthew 6:20–21

Introduction

What is a satisfied soul? you may be asking yourself. *And do I really want one?* Those are good questions.

Everyone looks for satisfaction in many ways and in many areas of their lives. We all want to feel fulfilled. But the person who experiences satisfaction on the job, in a marriage, and in other areas can remain empty if the soul remains confused, doubtful, or ignored.

Christians have learned that soul satisfaction is an unsurpassed delight, and it comes only from one place: Jesus. When we rest in Him, our spirits experience that long-sought fullness. Though it may be a challenge to do so, giving our lives entirely to Him to direct in whatever way He desires offers previously unimagined benefits.

Being a satisfied soul doesn't mean being self-satisfied—just the opposite. As believers, we find satisfaction in God, not our own efforts to gain His favor. Left to ourselves, our mechanical attempts to obey (because eventually we're bound to fall into automatic methods if we go our own way) fall short of His kingdom. As hard as we try, we don't have it in us to be perfect enough to deserve heaven. Only Jesus and the work of His Spirit in our lives can make the change we're really looking for.

Because the Christian life focuses on Jesus, and believers live out His broad blessings, in these pages you'll find many faith experiences: praise, joy, thanksgiving, overcoming, and so on. The satisfied soul is not a bored soul but one that experiences both good and bad and comes forth victorious in Jesus.

May this volume touch your life as you seek to be satisfied in Jesus. There's no one else who gives the full life you're looking for.

Satisfaction Guaranteed

Oh, satisfy us early with Your mercy,
that we may rejoice and be glad all our days!
PSALM 90:14 NKJV

You've probably bought items that guaranteed you'd be satisfied. If you weren't, the manufacturer promised you could get your money back. But how many people bought an item, weren't satisfied, and found the company didn't live up to that promise? Instead of money, all the customers got were irritating responses or rejection. A promise is only as good as the person or group who makes it. We've often found, to our discouragement, that people aren't what they seem and disappear as soon as they've cashed the check or processed the credit card information.

But God isn't like that. He's always what He says He is, and He's gone to great lengths to tell us about Himself. He sent prophets who wrote pages and pages about Him and His character. He even sent His Son to clearly show us what He's like. Jesus died for us to give a clear picture of how much He wanted to share our love.

Earthly guarantees often don't give us satisfaction, but when we read His Word and get to know His Son, we quickly comprehend the difference between people's promises and God's. His mercy doesn't fail us or make us miserable. As we accept it and live according to His promises, our joy increases, whatever turns life takes. Even when the rest of the world disappoints us, we can cling to Jesus and be glad to the very end.

Have you experienced God's mercy and responded to His love? Then your satisfaction is guaranteed. He promises you'll never be left or forsaken (Hebrews 13:5). Joy in Him will be your portion for the rest of your life.

Count Your Blessings

*Surely you have granted him unending
blessings and made him glad with
the joy of your presence.*

PSALM 21:6

"Count your blessings" is a popular phrase
I've never related well to. The moment I try
to list all God has done for me, I realize how
woefully short my efforts fall. I can thank Him
for my salvation and for the blessings of home,
relationships, work, and ministry. But I know
His grace extends far beyond that. Even if I
spent a week, I could hardly cover everything
adequately.

David didn't attempt to cram all God's
wonders in a single hymn. Though he rejoices
throughout Psalm 21, he hardly describes
everything God has done for him. The
king's adulation rings through much of the

psalter—as if he couldn't contain it in one place or time. But his masterful adoration is more than a list of thank-yous. David knew a secret of thanks it took me a while to uncover: real thanks are tied to the nature of God. Here David offers gratitude to his Lord for specific blessings in verses 1–6 and ends describing God's eternal gifts. All the psalmist's joy cannot be separated from his Master's presence. Without God, the king understands, even the richest gain would be empty. To know Him deeply is the greatest blessing of all, and intimate knowledge comes with a lifetime of loving Him.

So instead of detailing every benefit God provides, like David I'll thank Him for a few big ones today and spend time basking in His love. As I look closely into my Lord's face, I can't help but delight in His presence.

Best Love

Because your love is better than life,
my lips will glorify you.
PSALM 63:3

Nothing in this world is better than knowing God.

Perhaps, with all the delights of this world, that sounds a little strong. You may be in no rush to enter heaven and lose the things you've worked hard for and the earthly endowments God has given you. But if you can remember back to the days before you knew God, think of the difference He has made. Would you go back to life before Jesus? I know I wouldn't. The emptiness of life without Him is something I'd never want to reproduce. No wise Christian could trade anything for that kind of life.

Once Jesus enters a heart, losing life becomes but a painful moment that opens the door to eternity. When we know Him, we need no longer fear what happens after death. Eternal delights cannot compare to anything here on earth—even the best of the blessings God has already given us. Our hearts are no longer earthbound, and we long to be with Him. When He calls, we cannot imagine staying in this world without His blessing.

Though we may not rush to leave the fellowship of friends and family, the beauty of the world, and so much more that God has given, like the psalmist, we appreciate that anything that lacks Jesus is less than the best. Life here, without God's love, would be meaningless.

David had his priorities straight when he wrote this. Even being king of Israel, with all its benefits, wasn't better than loving God. So during his life, he praised his Maker. And in eternity, he's praising still.

Change of Mind

"For my thoughts are not your thoughts, neither are your ways my ways," declares the Lord.

Isaiah 55:8

I don't know why this verse always makes me think of an office gossipfest. Maybe it's because gossip is so clearly not something God engages in or because gossip is so hard to stop in its tracks. Perhaps it's also because the mentality that promotes it is so difficult to change, and it does so much damage to both the gossiper and the one talked about.

When I think of God's thoughts and mine, it's easy to imagine I'm naturally about as mentally delightful to God as a gossipfest. I fall short of what I should be. Not only can my speech be doubtful, but the actions that result from it can be far from godly. I'm sure many Christians have experienced the same weakness.

If God had left us in that situation, we'd be utterly miserable. Even our best efforts at change fail easily, no matter how much we want to be different. But God offers us His Spirit, not just as an encouragement, but as a heart changer. He enters into us and begins to redesign that gossiping speech. Suddenly, the things that come out of our mouths are truthful, kind, and fair. No longer do they reflect the blackness that painted our hearts but the rainbow colors of His blessings. Our ways too become His.

I'm glad God's thoughts and ways are different from mine. Without that difference, I'd be stuck in the muck of my own thinking, without escape. But today, I'm free to dwell in His thoughts and actions. There's no better way to live!

The Perfect Gift?

*Every good and perfect gift is from above,
coming down from the Father of the heavenly
lights, who does not change like shifting shadows.*
JAMES 1:17

Facing a challenge? It's easy to wonder, *Where
is God? Why did He allow this?* If your world
appears to be falling apart, it's tempting to decide
that God is ignoring you and even to wonder if
He's as benevolent as you thought.

James reminded the first-century church
that though circumstances changed, God didn't.
When these early believers faced trials—and
even death—they could trust that God was still
giving them good and perfect gifts.

It may not seem that way at the moment.
You may have lost a job or been forced to move
to a new location. Life seems out of control,
and stress threatens to overcome you. You can't

see a good thing about it. But wait awhile. In a year or two, when you look back on this, God's plan may seem clearer. Maybe the new job will prove better than the old, or the challenge will give you new skills to further your career. The new place, once you adapt to it, may also bring you stronger friends, a better church, and an improved life.

Don't judge God's gifts until you have unwrapped the whole package. Often His presents are larger than they seem and take longer to unpack than you thought. But in the end, you're likely to learn that whatever pain you put into the situation is much less than His blessing—and without that pain, you'd never have had all God wanted to give you.

See, the gift really was perfect after all, and God didn't stop being good. For a while, you just couldn't see through the wrapping paper.

Peace Accord

*Let the peace that comes from Christ rule in
your hearts. For as members of one body you are
called to live in peace. And always be thankful.*
COLOSSIANS 3:15 NLT

Any collection of people who have a gripe,
unsolved problem, or major disagreement keep
coming back to it in many ways—they cannot
live quietly with an unsettled issue. But bringing
peace isn't as easy as it might seem on paper.
The emotions that accompany disagreement
can keep peace at bay for a long time.

Even in the church, peace can be hard won.
You know that if you belong to one involved in
an emotional struggle. If you don't have more
than doctrine in common, your congregation
is in trouble.

Paul defines what we need in order to have
peace: a heart change that gives us "tenderhearted

mercy, kindness, humility, gentleness, and patience" (Colossians 3:12 NLT). But even our best efforts to make peace fail when, as hard as we try to forgive, resentment resurfaces in our hearts. Suddenly, we recognize that our deceitful hearts refuse to go in the direction our heads tell us to travel. No matter how hard we try, we can't make our own accord, because though logic tells us to do right, our emotions head off in the wrong direction.

The only way to find real peace is through the one Jesus offers. Only He can make His Word truly rule our hearts, not through empty doctrines we cannot perform but through a whole-heart desire to serve Him only and love others through Him. The compassion, forgiveness, and love that escaped us dwell firmly in us when we submit to His will.

That peace not only affects us body and soul, it makes us thankful for God's work in our hearts and lives. Finally, we feel peace in every part.

Mission Impossible?

*Husbands, love your wives
and never treat them harshly.*
COLOSSIANS 3:19 NLT

The "battle of the sexes" pits men and women against each other. Even in the church, spouses attempt to make each other fulfill their "roles" by using verses like this against each other. Somehow I don't think that's what Paul or God had in mind when these words were written down for all humanity. I'm certain it wasn't what God created marriage to be.

Let's not forget, when we read this verse, that God is the One who enables the sexes to live in this kind of accord. He wouldn't command husbands to do the impossible, though He might give them a hard task. Anything He asks a Christian to do, He also provides power to accomplish. There's no Mission Impossible with God.

I have to admit, I don't understand how God does it. But I've learned in my own marriage that taking any problem to Him in prayer can be the start of big changes. When my husband and I face the seemingly impossible and together share it with God, the way suddenly becomes smoother. Bumps we expected in our road never appear, or we manage to circumnavigate the worst of them. Solutions we'd never expected suddenly become plain. Things are never worse than I expected, after we share our way with God.

I want to thank God for a godly husband who has made loving me a priority. Embittered disagreements aren't part of our lifestyle because he's committed to love his Savior.

But God didn't end it there. He made this marriage mission more than possible. When we live in Him, it becomes fun too.

A Challenging Love

Love does no wrong to others, so love fulfills the requirement of God's law.

ROMANS 13:10 NLT

Loving your neighbor as yourself, Jesus said, was the second greatest commandment, following only the command to love God completely. Then He commented that all scripture was based on these truths (Matthew 22:37–40).

Loving God isn't hard to understand, even when we struggle to perfect our love. Though we often don't comprehend Jesus, we can accept that He's bigger and greater than we are, and He knows what's best for us.

But loving a neighbor, especially a difficult one, can be a real challenge. Will the action we're contemplating do harm to her? Will telling a family member what we think or how he's hurt us just cause more trouble or bring the resolution we've been seeking? Even when we want to do right, we often struggle with the details.

Love comes in many packages. If we need to hold back a harsh word, that's love. But love can also mean speaking the truth kindly and gently, at a moment when a friend or family member is willing to hear. How can we tell which is necessary?

Before we take an action, we can begin by testing our own hearts. Is there bitterness or criticism there? Then we cannot fulfill God's law. Are we suiting this simply to our own sense of timing, when another is not ready to listen? Then God is not likely to be pleased with that action.

Love looks more to the needs of others than ourselves. It takes into account their hearts, minds, and souls. Fulfilling the law is never easy for humans. It takes a God-sized heart to do that well—that's why we can only do it through Jesus.

Protection Expectations

God is our refuge and strength,
a very present help in trouble.
PSALM 46:1 KJV

I refer to our male basset hound, Belvedere, as our policeman. When I take him for a walk, he warns me of "trouble"—a dog walking across the street, a neighbor getting in a car, or a package being delivered. But barking at these less-than-dangerous things is really all he's good for. As soon as a person or animal comes close, he wants to make friends. His bark is loud and scary, but there isn't a bit of bite in him. My neighbors just laugh at his noise because they know how much it means. And if any trouble threatened, I'm sure Bel would be the one hiding behind me instead of being a "help in trouble."

Though we may not seriously look to dogs

to fulfill our protection expectations, whether or not we realize it, we all have them. We expect the police to intervene if a robber threatens our home—and hope they will catch him. We expect our bosses not to allow anything harmful in our workplaces and take them to task if they do. But no matter how many efforts anyone takes, human effort never fully defends us from harm. Storms come and damage our land. Terrorists attack. No defense is perfect.

Only one Protector keeps us really safe, whether it's from physical harm, emotional hurt, or a spiritual temptation. Only One aids us in our pain, in the middle of the day or the wee hours of the night. Jesus is no mere barking dog but true protection from trouble and a companion in every trial. When we can't rely on a hound or a human, He'll stand by us faithfully.

Thankful Prayer

*So that you may live a life worthy
of the Lord and please him in every
way: bearing fruit in every good work,
growing in the knowledge of God.*

COLOSSIANS 1:10

If your pastor commended your church the way Paul praised the Colossians (1:3–8), you'd feel pretty proud of yourselves. But even while you were appreciating the encouragement on how faithful you'd remained, you'd probably understand that it wasn't the end of your Christian walk. The apostle didn't stop there— and neither would your pastor. Instead of assuming that the people of this church would never fail in their belief, Paul kept on praying that they'd know God's will and understand it (Colossians 1:9).

Doing okay for the moment, as far as Paul

was concerned, was not enough for Christians. He rejoiced in the church's growth, but he didn't encourage successful believers to rest on their laurels. In the spiritual life, things always change. New challenges arise, and God ordains additional growth every day for His children. Just when any of us think we've got things under control, Satan launches another attack or God ordains a challenging service. No one can stop doing God's will and remain a faithful Christian. So though Paul was thankful, he asked God to keep the Colossians' spiritual lives moving forward.

When you've done well in your walk, be thankful that God's Spirit kept you faithful. Appreciate anyone who has helped you along the way. Then, don't sit back and imagine that you're at the peak of your Christian faithfulness. For the growing Christian, there are always new opportunities to know Jesus and bear fruit that pleases Him. Keep on growing in Him today.

Spiritual Competition?

*I always thank my God for you because
of his grace given you in Christ Jesus.*
1 CORINTHIANS 1:4

When God gives another, younger Christian a great blessing, are you thankful or jealous? Paul felt thankful that a powerful blessing had fallen on the Corinthians. Though they were still young believers and didn't have it all together, the correction Paul administered in this letter was not done from a sense of jealousy. A few verses later, the apostle lets them know he isn't interested in making himself famous but in lifting up Jesus. From one who had worked to develop thriving churches on two continents, his sense of humility is amazing.

God doesn't give any of us blessings to start a game of "Who Can Top This?" A competition for "spiritual position" just isn't part of His plan. Realizing the futility of such desires, Paul committed himself to doing the real job—reaching people for Jesus—instead of trying to make himself look good.

How many of our churches could learn from Paul's example? So often we could benefit from following in his footsteps, lifting up others who are new to the faith and need encouragement, as well as another lesson in what it means to love Jesus.

Are there new Christians in your church who are doing great things for God, even though they don't know the scriptures as well as you do? Come alongside them and encourage them. Offer to help them however you can. Make it a priority to pray for them. Then thank God for the blessings He's given you too, and make the most of your gifts so that together you can lead people to Jesus.

Never Give Up

Grace and peace to you from God our Father and the Lord Jesus Christ.

1 CORINTHIANS 1:3

If anyone really needed grace and peace, it was the Corinthians. Paul's letters to them describe a church that constantly faced problems that might make a lot of modern-day believers move to another congregation. Sin didn't creep into that church; it marched right up and took charge.

Yet when the apostle wished grace and peace on these young Christians, he wasn't being facetious. The first eight verses of this chapter make that clear. Paul was more interested in putting them on the right path than handing them a harsh critique. Any critical comments are designed to show them a better way in Jesus.

We too may have days when we need

huge quantities of God's grace and peace. A relationship gone awry, a bad choice that we have to live with, or a seemingly impossible work situation has derailed our lives. We know what's wrong, and we're not looking for anyone to simply delight in telling us how bad we are. Instead, we need a solution.

Like those Corinthians, when we get help, we'll have to face the bad news and admit what wrongs we've done. But we also need someone like Paul, who won't give up on us. We want one of God's people to come to us with grace and peace, help us find the right path, and aid us in walking down it for the rest of our lives.

No Christian is beyond God's grace and peace. Paul told that to the Corinthians, and he's telling it to us too. Jesus picks up fallen people with His unending grace and mercy. He never, never, never gives up on a child who calls out to Him.

The Greatest Reward

*Therefore do not cast away your
confidence, which has great reward.*
HEBREWS 10:35 NKJV

In the working world, confidence gets a lot
of appreciation. If you seem to think well of
yourself, can stand up to opposition, and deal
well with others, you're likely to get ahead.
Those who are shy and uncertain of their own
abilities have a harder time making it up the
corporate ladder.

The rewards of social confidence can seem
impressive. It may bring a larger car or house,
increased social connections, and more work-
related responsibilities. But none of those things
is the "great reward" this scripture speaks of.
The writer of Hebrews is talking about the final
spiritual reward of heaven. To his readers, who
struggled in a world where their confidence in

Jesus was not popular, the truth that faith brings a reward far beyond any social skill was more of a lifesaver than a rescue helicopter to a person adrift in a choppy sea. As they felt themselves going down for the third time, God reminded them that even going down in this world didn't settle things in the next one.

Like those fearful first-century Christians, if we believe in Jesus, we've been cast a lifeline. We've connected ourselves to Him in faith, and though we struggle to work out our beliefs with consistency, our hearts are truly His. That internal confidence earned us the greatest reward: eternity with our Savior.

There's nothing wrong with having a healthy degree of self-confidence; in fact, building your faith may also build up your ability to think properly of yourself. But no matter how many social skills you develop, don't trust in them alone. Because everything they offer will be here today and gone in eternity. Only faith in Jesus lasts forever.

Define Slow

The Lord is not slow in keeping his promise, as some understand slowness. Instead he is patient with you, not wanting anyone to perish, but everyone to come to repentance.

2 PETER 3:9

Time may drag as you're waiting for God to aid you in changing a bad habit or to bring newness to a difficult relationship. You begin to wonder if He'll ever intervene. Then when you least expect it, He brings wonderful change into your life. Was God slow? No, He just had another plan, and when the time was perfect, He did what you'd asked for.

It's the same, Peter told his readers, with the day of the Lord, the time when Jesus will return for His people. Because it hadn't happened on these first-century believers' schedule, they began to doubt the promise. When nonbelievers scoffed at their faith, the Christians asked, "Why is God so slow?"

Peter assured them God had not forgotten His people or His promise. He simply had a better plan—one that would add many others to the kingdom. As it turned out, Jesus didn't return during their century. But that doesn't mean He wasn't faithful. Though the early Christians might have been stunned that God would wait so long, they couldn't have argued with the need for many others to come to Him.

It's all a matter of how we define slow. If it means "anything that doesn't fit into our schedules," we would consider God slow. But if it means "something behind God's schedule," the word can't be used about God's plan. He's never behind on His own timetable. So, no, God isn't slow in coming—or in doing anything else in our lives. The real question is: "Are we on God's schedule or our own?"

Deep Roots

*Blessed is the one who. . .is like a tree
planted by streams of water, which yields
its fruit in season and whose leaf does not
wither—whatever they do prospers.*
PSALM 1:1, 3

What a delightful picture of a faithful person:
a well-watered tree that never drops its leaves.
It's easy to imagine a large tree, spreading wide
and bearing plentifully. We'd like to be like that
tree, sending our roots deep into life and finding
a lot of prosperity.

So why don't Christians stand head and
shoulders above other people in this world?
Maybe it's because not many of us do what
the rest of this psalm says—we don't avoid
the wicked and their ways; we don't delight in
God's Word. We don't feed our tree with the
right things. Instead of giving it pure water

from the scriptures, we allow it to drink in lies. So it begins to lose a few leaves, and we ignore them, below our boughs. We settle for a little fruit instead of a complete harvest.

That's not the way it has to be. It isn't what God designed for us. That's why He gave the psalmist this description, to challenge believers to be steadfast in their faith. None of us needs to settle for a second-best Christianity.

If we have been faithful, let us challenge ourselves to become more so. And if we doubt that God has made us prosper, let us consider what prosperity means. Are we looking for more money and a bigger car or deeper faithfulness to Him? Which will shine brighter in eternity—the polish on that car or a life that gleams for Him?

Satisfied Souls

May God himself, the God of peace, sanctify
you through and through. May your whole
spirit, soul and body be kept blameless at the
coming of our Lord Jesus Christ.

1 THESSALONIANS 5:23

Ah, this is the picture of a satisfied soul. Made holy through and through, the believer rests in Jesus. That Christian can look forward to standing before God, satisfied that every necessary mission is accomplished.

It's not by chance that Paul puts this comment at the end of 1 Thessalonians. He's already shared his message describing how the Christians of Thessalonica can obey God. He's written about the Lord's coming, given instructions on Christian living, and warned them to avoid evil. But Paul isn't promising them a future sitting on their laurels, doing nothing but singing psalms. God's battle against evil has only begun. Paul asks that He will continue to make them holy through whatever challenges lie ahead. Knowing God will be faithful to all His people, Paul looks past the challenges believers face on earth to the final outcome of faith.

We might like to think Christianity has more hours of laurel sitting than battle. None of us prefers hard work to the blessings of peace, yet we can't have one without the other. God's sanctification is worked out in our lives with effort, and no one achieves spiritual growth only by singing psalms. That restful part of our lives blesses us between the battles that put sin in its proper place—behind us.

One day, we won't have to settle for brief spells of satisfaction. We'll spend all eternity singing God's praises for the victories He gave us on earth. Our mission accomplished, we'll fill heaven with the rejoicing of satisfied souls.

Awesome Deeds

*You faithfully answer our prayers with
awesome deeds, O God our savior.
You are the hope of everyone on earth.*
PSALM 65:5 NLT

Prayer life feeling a little lackluster? Then read
this verse. Mull it over a bit and trust that God
really means what He says. Awesome deeds?
In response to our prayers? Why don't we
frequently receive responses like that? Maybe
we'd better take another look at this praying
thing.

Obviously, when we hope for an awesome
response to our communication with God,
it's not because we're so wonderful. Finding
the perfect way to ask won't work—that's
expecting magic, not faith. But somehow, as
we do ordinary petitioning, God provides the
wonderful answers.

David doesn't talk much in this psalm about the qualities of himself. Instead he is simply lost in awe at how wonderful the Lord is, and that's the right focus for prayer. As long as we puff ourselves up, talk to God about how wonderful we are or all the plans we have for our spiritual lives, our faith goes nowhere. We were never meant to be the focus of prayer. Our petty concerns pale beside the abilities and plans of our heavenly Father, who made heaven, earth, and even us. Prayer without worship may feel good to us, but it simply hits the ceiling. No wonder we don't get much response.

But when we treat God as if He really is our hope on earth, praise Him for His wonderful deeds, and worship Him, the awesome deeds can begin—the change in us is only the beginning!

Second Time Around

Then the word of the LORD came to Jonah a second time: "Go to the great city of Nineveh and proclaim to it the message I give you."

JONAH 3:1–2

Does God have to tell you a second time, like Jonah, or do you listen when He first asks you to take on a difficult task for Him?

It's not hard to understand Jonah's refusal. God wanted to send His prophet to the capital of Assyria, Israel's enemy. This extremely violent nation, expert at wiping out other countries, was the war machine of the day, and other countries feared it for good reason. They were not nice people. But Jonah knew his compassionate God and feared that instead of punishing the wicked Assyrians, He would forgive them. Preferring his enemies in hell, the prophet refused to do God's command.

What was Jonah thinking? we ask ourselves. *Didn't he know God is in control of everything, and if He wants people saved, they will be?* It's so easy to see the story clearly when it's from another person's perspective. But we've done it ourselves, haven't we? God asks us to speak to a person about Him, and we keep putting it off. We'll do it "someday." He asks us to begin a ministry and we resist, figuring we're not "spiritual" enough.

When we respond like Jonah, we may end up in a painful situation. We probably won't enter a fish's belly, but trouble can still find us for a while. In the end, God will bring us to do His will after all. He gives a second chance, and we'll obey this time—unless we prefer sitting in the twenty-first-century equivalent of a fish belly.

Covered with Sackcloth?

*"But let people and animals be covered
with sackcloth. Let everyone call urgently
on God. Let them give up their evil
ways and their violence."*

JONAH 3:8

The Assyrians had a lot to repent for. When
this violent, wicked people heard about their
upcoming destruction by God, Jonah's words
hit their hearts. They couldn't seem to ask
forgiveness fast enough. Their king demanded
that even the beasts be covered with sackcloth,
a rough, uncomfortable fabric that indicated
repentance.

I don't know about your animals, but I
certainly doubt my basset hounds' ability to
repent. When I catch one of them in wrongdoing,
I get that mournful look many people mistake
for "feeling sorry," but I'm not fooled. I know
that if they're sorry, it's because they got caught,

not because they have some finer moral feeling. Chances are that I will catch that hound in the same kind of act within the next week—if not the next day! Getting an animal to "repent" and change actions is more a matter of training than appealing to a higher moral code.

Why did the king cover animals in sackcloth? Because he was trying to show a total repentance that might encourage God to forgive them. The king wanted nothing between his nation and God's mercy.

We don't cover our cats and dogs in sackcloth or make a new covering for the bird's cage. Because we appreciate God's generous mercy, we know He's not going to blame our animals or wipe us out because they didn't appear properly repentant. But do we also appreciate the mercy that saved us from as much destruction as the Assyrians? Do we feel the joyful thanks of those ancient people and live in a way that shows our appreciation?

If not, maybe we'd better search out sackcloth for our hearts.

Abundant Life

> *"The thief's purpose is to steal and kill and destroy. My purpose is to give them a rich and satisfying life."*
>
> JOHN 10:10 NLT

Abundant life, full of good things on this earth, spiritual peace and joy, and full, satisfying relationships—that's what God intends His people to have. But listen to the world, and you'd never know it. Non-Christians often portray Christians as narrow-minded, sad, or hopelessly idealistic.

That's probably not the faith you know. Because Jesus entered your life, you've entered a new realm—and it's not the Twilight Zone either. Life has taken on a new meaning because you know the Creator. You feel clean, right with your Maker, and richer for being in a relationship with Him. Though you're far from perfect, He's been working in your life to bring spiritual abundance, deeper understanding of Him and the world around you, and a joy that doesn't stop when trouble enters the door.

Nonbelievers can't know any of that. You can tell them that loving Jesus is the best thing ever, and they'll wonder if you're zany. They've never experienced anything like it, so they can't imagine such peace and joy. And whatever we've never felt for ourselves, we humans tend to doubt.

But one day the thief who comes to steal, kill, and destroy their lives makes them so miserable that God's message enters a crack in their armor against Him. They start to listen to His message of abundant life, and before long faith blossoms, breaking open the hardware that kept abundance at bay. New life, abundant life, takes hold.

It's time to rejoice in Jesus.

What's in a Name?

*"Until now you have not asked for anything
in my name. Ask and you will receive,
and your joy will be complete."*

JOHN 16:24

Has anyone ever asked anything in your name?
Perhaps your child invoked your name when
seeking help from one of your friends. "I'm Terry
Smith's daughter," or "I'm Kathy Moore's son."
Chances are, your friend was quickly ready to
help. Because that person knew you, your child
was important.

It's the same when we go to God and pray
in Jesus' name. God recognizes that we have
received His forgiveness through His Son, and
He's happy to grant us our wishes. He gives
good things that make us happy.

But that doesn't mean He gives us everything
we ask for. If your child tried to borrow a million

dollars from your friend, but your friend knew your credit didn't run that high, no money would be forthcoming. The request wouldn't be like you—wouldn't fit with your personality and abilities. In the same way, the requests we place before God have to "look" like Jesus. If we ask for something that isn't part of Him—if it's a selfish request or aimed at wrongdoing—we won't get it.

But when we ask in Jesus' will—for an ailing friend who needs healing, a relative who doesn't have salvation and is desperately seeking, or our own spiritual growth—God is happy to give. Only instead of looking just the way we expect, our answer may take a different form. That's because all of our answers have to look just like Jesus.

Good Gift?

"If you then, being evil, know how to give good gifts to your children, how much more will your Father who is in heaven give good things to those who ask Him!"

MATTHEW 7:11 NKJV

Ever wonder if the things God was giving you were all good? As you faced a trial, perhaps you wanted to know what He had in mind. Or maybe your child came home with a trouble while you were in the middle of your own crisis, and you wondered, *Why me, Lord?*

It's not unusual for us to question our trials. If we went out looking for troubles, we'd be masochists—naturally, we'd prefer to avoid all the problems we can. Sensibly, we make efforts to make our lives smooth and prosperous.

So when we've been praying faithfully, seeking God's will, and trying our best, but trouble still afflicts us, maybe it isn't all evil. Instead, God might have a blessing that can only come when we've been tested. That struggling child may need attention during his challenging situation, but it may become the key to a better relationship.

Even in the midst of our worst troubles, we can trust that, as Jesus said, God still remembers how to give good gifts. Though we don't like our situations, God's ability to give good things hasn't dried up. And as we cannot forget our children, how much less can He erase our relationship from His memory?

If we, who lack all God's powers, do good things for those we love, how much more is He willing to do them for us? All we need to do is trust that something good lies at the end of this trial—something God had in mind for us all along.

All Good

For everything God created is good,
and nothing is to be rejected if it is
received with thanksgiving.
1 TIMOTHY 4:4

God didn't create anything that wasn't good, Paul stated emphatically in the face of heretical teachers who wanted to deny Christians everything from marriage to meat. The apostle made it clear that God didn't tease us by putting extra temptations in the world—denying us the best it had to offer.

Has God given you good things? In our culture, that often implies a huge house, a fancy car, and steak for dinner. But haven't you had a house you loved, even though it wasn't in the finest part of town, an older car you didn't want to get rid of, or a macaroni-and-cheese dinner that fed your stomach and your taste buds as well as any steak? Good things don't have to cost a lot of money.

Your best relationships are priceless. Would you trade a much-loved parent for money or a spouse for gold? These too are gifts from the heavenly Father, who knows how to give the best—no matter the cost.

And what of the other things God creates that have no price? A sunset filled with vibrant colors, a nighttime sky that shades from light to darkest blue and is sprinkled with glowing stars, a drink of water that quenches thirst as no man-made beverage can. God has given generously in many more ways than we often consider.

But no matter what God gives us, whether it's a no-frills economy car or a luxury coupe, a filet mignon or chicken, we are to receive it with thanks. He made it just for us, and we're enjoying the benefit, so why not share that joy with Jesus? He's the best gift God had to offer—and we didn't reject it either.

Excellent Things

"Sing to the LORD, for He has done excellent things; this is known in all the earth."
ISAIAH 12:5 NKJV

Excellent things! God doesn't just do good things or the best things. He does *excellent* things. What could improve on God's superb plan or will? But do we appreciate what He has done for us?

This verse comes from a prophetic praise that looks forward to the day of the Lord. In the return of the Messiah, when the Israelites see their salvation, Isaiah promises they will appreciate the excellent things He has done for them. The doubts they had here on earth will all be swept away as they understand and praise Him.

But God had already done many wonderful things for His people—they had been brought out of bondage and into the Promised Land, and He'd made Israel great under King David. But when they became unfaithful, they fell into weakness, and the Assyrians overcame their small country. No longer could they appreciate God's excellence and all He'd done for them. Blinded by sin to His greatness, most could not appreciate Him. Only a few remaining faithful ones were left to claim that God was still doing excellent things.

Are our eyes open to the excellent things He's done for His people—and is still doing for them today? We have seen the fulfillment of the Messianic prophecies that precede this verse and felt the impact of His salvation. We know much that was hidden to the ancient Israelites. Yet sin can blind our eyes too.

Have we thanked God for the excellent things of the past and present? Are we looking forward to the joys of the future? Have we truly appreciated Him in prayer and praise?

God's Friend

"But you, Israel, my servant, Jacob,
whom I have chosen, you descendants of
Abraham my friend, I took you from the ends
of the earth, from its farthest corners I called
you. I said, 'You are my servant'; I have
chosen you and have not rejected you."

ISAIAH 41:8–9

Have you pondered the idea that, like Israel, the Lord of the universe is your friend? Perhaps you've been stopped in your tracks by the awe of that truth. *Why should He care for me?* you may wonder.

God chooses His friends on His own terms. The famous, the extraordinarily intelligent, the powerful aren't always on His list. Yet some of the most unexpected folks are. He doesn't choose based on worldly greatness (He doesn't need it, because He has enough greatness of

His own). His own sense of mercy defines the choice in ways we cannot now understand.

Many blessings follow friendship with God, but so do challenges. The Creator expects much of His friends, just as He gives much. He doesn't ask just anyone to take on the job, which also requires training in faithfulness. Anyone not willing to do His will need not apply for the position. Being a friend of Jesus requires that we suffer, struggle, and face numerous challenges, physically and spiritually. It's not the kind of thing He offers lightly or we should accept blindly.

But when God chooses a friend, it's forever. He never gives up or changes His mind. He's with you for this lifetime and eternity. Along with all the purely delightful things in His hand, He offers strength in trials and guidance for a long, hard way. Nothing that happens is beyond His strength or help.

That's the best friendship anyone could offer.

Pleasurable Days

*Remember now your Creator in the days
of your youth, before the difficult days come,
and the years draw near when you say,
"I have no pleasure in them."*
ECCLESIASTES 12:1 NKJV

Good news! You don't have to wait until you're old and gray to come to God and receive His blessings. He wants even young people to accept Him. No one can say that you are too young to know Jesus. In fact, statistics show that most people come to Him by age eighteen. God loves young people.

Maybe that's partly because He doesn't want to see people suffer unnecessarily. Instead of leaving them to work out their lives in their own ways, fall into sin, and make a mess of things, He wants to guide them in the choice of a mate, a career, and a lifestyle. He wants to shower many blessings on them for a lifetime instead of limiting His impact to a few years. As He touches their lives early, He knows they will have better, more enjoyable lives—and lives that glorify Him longer.

You don't have to be facing the end of your life to be blessed by Jesus. He wants to bless you today. Whether you are under eighteen, just over it, or several decades beyond, He wants to share His love for as many years as you'll let Him.

Before sin has squeezed the pleasure from your days, trouble has furrowed your brow, and your relationships seem more trouble than they're worth, turn to Jesus. When you face difficult days, as all people do, you won't stand alone. Trouble won't blast your life but will strengthen you instead. Your Creator can turn all trials to blessings, if you just stand firm in Him.

Enjoy your days in Jesus.

Love Life

The Lord is far from the wicked,
but He hears the prayer of the righteous.
PROVERBS 15:29 NKJV

From one year to another, a man who doesn't love God doesn't pray until a loved one becomes ill. Then the desperate unbeliever may decide to give prayer a try. But if God doesn't respond "properly," by saving the ill one, he complains God doesn't exist or doesn't care about people.

What that weak prayer doesn't understand is that God doesn't have to respond to every petition. Praying is part of an intimate relationship with Him, and anyone who attempts to ask for blessings apart from that relationship is coming to a complete stranger and asking for great wealth. Trading on the goodwill of someone you don't know is a risky business, and in this context, it's not one God encourages.

Yet the one who does not know Him is not entirely without hope. Jesus calls people to come to Him in repentance. The woman in trouble who admits her need of the Savior suddenly realizes that God does answer prayer. Though He may not respond the way she expected, great blessing can follow, even in the midst of terrible trial.

God loves to listen to His people, and when have you heard a Christian complain about having prayed too much? In a deep, caring relationship, neither party can speak too much to the other. Just as a man and woman who have newly discovered love discuss all their joys and cares, the Christian shares everything with the Lord.

Has prayer become mechanical, a chore instead of a joy? Remember how beloved you are by the One you're speaking to. He doesn't want to hear the details of just anyone's life— He's asked you to share with Him, and you're blessed to know His love.

On High Places

He [God] makes my feet like the feet of deer,
and sets me on my high places.
PSALM 18:33 NKJV

Like a bounding deer, the believer who trusts in
God jumps from rock to rock, unfazed by the
hardness underfoot. What a lovely image David
gave us in this psalm describing the blessings
God offers to those who trust entirely in Him.

If only we could trust God perfectly each day
and rise constantly up, higher on the mountain.
We'd like to think that's an ideal Christian
experience. But our spiritual landscape does
not consist simply of mountains. Valleys lie
between the uplands, as David attested when
he wrote: "Though I walk through the valley
of the shadow of death" (Psalm 23:4 NKJV).
And without those valleys, there would be no
mountains at all.

All believers, spiritual giants like David or those of more average size, cannot forever rise above trouble. Until we live in a heavenly world, a fallen world's hardships impact us. However, whether we set our feet on high places or valleys, one thing remains the same. When David wrote about God's blessing in helping us overcome trouble or about the joy of completed overcoming, he realized one truth. Challenges that threaten to undo us or joy at overcoming share one thing: God never leaves us in either situation. "I will fear no evil; for You are with me," Psalm 23:4 (NKJV) continues. And 2 Samuel 22:51 concludes, "He gives his king great victories."

So whether we're bounding along in faith or struggling through a doleful valley, our faith does not change. We still trust in the One who made both mountains and valleys, and He'll faithfully see us through either.

Awed!

Great is the Lord and most worthy of praise;
his greatness no one can fathom.
PSALM 145:3

If you've ever tried to follow a man-made philosophy, you've discovered its limitations. As time went on, you found problems it couldn't solve or simply ignored because it had no answers. Even the "best" people can only take on so many issues—in their own power they can only do so much. Their greatness only goes so far.

But that's not true of God. No matter how many issues we bring to Him, He has an answer. No matter how low our lives seem to go, He can bring us up again. We see His hand at work in the nations or the minutia of our lives, and in both He remains faithful. Nothing lies beyond His grasp.

We may pride ourselves on being "scientific people," but what we call science is simply our understanding of His creation. We only comprehend a small part of His inventive mind. Despite centuries of study, we've just scratched the very surface of the world He made to share with us.

As we look at God's greatness and experience His love, awe fills our beings. Our scant ability to appreciate His personality and power lays bare our own smallness. Yet when the Creator points out their frailty to His faithful ones, He's not belittling us. He simply shares the truth of His own character. He reminds us that He also wants to share all He has and all He is with us. Instead of hoarding all He is and making us pay the price for our own weakness, He mercifully sent His Son to share all with us.

Could anything be greater or so deserve our awed praise?

Too Hard?

"Is anything too hard for the LORD?
I will return to you at the appointed time
next year, and Sarah will have a son."

GENESIS 18:14

Is there something in your life that seems too hard even for God to deal with? A relationship turned sour, a work-related situation, a financial trouble? You've asked God for a solution, and it hasn't appeared quickly. So maybe, like Abraham and Sarah, you've been looking elsewhere for the answers.

God had promised this elderly couple a son. The idea thrilled them—an heir to take over the family business after Abraham died, a child to fill the empty arms of Sarah, who had struggled with barrenness. But time went on, and no son appeared, so they took matters into their own hands and tried to make this child of promise.

Hagar, Sarah's servant, bore Abraham's son. But Ishmael still wasn't the child God promised. Tension filled their camp instead of the peace that follows God's will.

Though the people weren't faithful, God was. They tried to do things their way, but it didn't change His promise. God wanted them to have a blessing, so He still sent the promised son, Isaac.

It's the same with the people He blesses today. We may decide a situation is impossible, run into trouble, and forget God. But He doesn't forget us. He still wants to bless us, and He will, but perhaps He has to get our attention first. As long as we're heading in the opposite direction, even if we received a blessing, we wouldn't appreciate it. Even the best God could give would become mired in our disobedience.

God wants to bless you today. Are you ready to receive all the good He has to offer?

Jesus Cares

LORD, be gracious to us; we long for
you. Be our strength every morning,
our salvation in time of distress.
ISAIAH 33:2

Need strength? Require help? They're not far from you. Look no further than your Savior. No matter what's going on in your life, He's always there, waiting for you to turn to Him.

Unlike Isaiah's contemporaries, you may not be facing overwhelming armies, ready to take your country hostage, but your daily challenges are still important to Jesus. Like the prophet, you can call on Him, no matter what you face. In fact, God tells you to share all your troubles with Him because He cares for you (1 Peter 5:7). That means He's concerned about all the things you face, day by day, all the trials and troubles, everything that impacts your life.

On that tired morning, when it's hard to get moving, you can call on Jesus. When a life-changing problem looms ahead in your day, He cares about that too. Can you find a problem He tells you to take somewhere else? No. He told you to give Him *all* your troubles, and He means just that. Whether it's a son or daughter who's hard to handle, a difficulty on the job, or a spiritual issue you can't seem to resolve, He offers both a listening ear and answers.

Do you long for help from God? Your desire is in the right place. Just ask then trust He will answer. Tomorrow may not solve every problem, but you can know that help is on the way. You've put your faith in the eternal God who never fails. Talk to Him this morning and watch help appear.

Immediate Blessings

However, as it is written: "What no eye has seen, what no ear has heard, and what no human mind has conceived"—the things God has prepared for those who love him.

1 Corinthians 2:9

God has future blessings in mind for you, but did you realize that this verse is also talking about things you can experience today? Read the context of this passage, and you'll notice that Paul isn't talking about the sweet by-and-by—he's describing his current ministry and the work of the Spirit in the lives of Christians.

So if you've been waiting for heaven to enjoy all the joys and delights of faith, turn around. Look at the blessings you've received today, all the things God has done and is doing in your life, and appreciate them. But don't stop there; you can also start taking advantage of the spiritual mission God has given you. Because God never gives us blessings simply to enjoy—every good thing is meant to be shared.

You don't have to look to another Christian to discover what God has for you. No one in this world can tell you what He has in mind. Verse 10 says God reveals these unseen gifts by His Spirit. So don't hunt through the church, compare your assets to your friends', or even search the world for God's blessings. You won't find them.

Go to the real source—God. He may not share your blessings with the world, but He wants to share them with you. If you ask, He'll show you what He's given and how He wants you to impact others with them.

He has wonderful things in mind for you, so don't wait until eternity—share some of that good news today!

Additions and Subtractions

*Do not add to what I command you and do
not subtract from it, but keep the commands
of the Lord your God that I give you.*

DEUTERONOMY 4:2

My computer grammar check didn't like this
verse. It wanted to delete the "not" before
"subtract." If I didn't know better, I'd think
I had a real person in there, objecting to the
meaning of this passage, someone who wanted
to change the upcoming Ten Commandments.
Perhaps he'd like to get rid of the prohibition
against adultery or the command not to have
idols. Then he'd be able to do what he wanted
and ignore the guilt.

The truth of the matter is, keeping God's
Word isn't always easy. Sometimes we'd all
like to take out a passage here or there. We'd
like to modify some verses to seem less

harsh—or less merciful. Or we'd like to add something we think is better. It's not the things we don't understand in the Bible that bother us as much as the things we do understand and don't want to agree with.

But God didn't give us His Word to edit— He gave it as a blessing that will show us how to live. With it we can avoid trouble and receive all the good things God has for us. His commands aren't open to a lot of doubting. They are not unclear, open to differences of opinion, or questionable. These ten quick takes on what it means to believe form the basis for a valuable spiritual life.

So instead of editing or rewriting, let's obey. Before long, we won't be questioning, doubting, or disagreeing. Instead we'll be praising God for the work He's done in our lives because we followed His Word just as He commanded.

Good Friends

Don't visit your neighbors too often,
or you will wear out your welcome.
PROVERBS 25:17 NLT

Not only does God want to bless us, He wants us to share that blessing. But in His infinite wisdom, He knows our well-meaning efforts can go awry. It may happen when we first receive Christ and are anxious for our friends to do so too. We may constantly visit, hoping to show them the joys of God. Or when we move to a new place and don't know many people, we may become dependent on the first people we meet. Eventually, our company becomes tiresome, and even the best of friends wants a rest. If someone asks for space, it doesn't mean she doesn't care but that she needs a rest from our company so she can give her energies to other life demands. Given space, that friendship may actually grow stronger.

Being a good friend and neighbor doesn't require constant togetherness but does need constant love. Sometimes that means not seeing a friend for a while because he's busy at the office. Or she may have a new romance she's spending a lot of time on. Because you don't see your friend every day doesn't mean either of you doesn't care.

Because God cares about us, He gives us tools to build good relationships. This is one of them. If we're wise, we'll heed His Word and make use of this truth to strengthen friendships. Then we'll be in a good position to share our faith with those who don't know Jesus or to encourage our siblings in Christ. And that will be a real blessing.

Fishing Practice

Love suffers long and is kind; love does not envy;
love does not parade itself, is not puffed up.

1 CORINTHIANS 13:4 NKJV

Fly-fishing is really quite easy—if you buy the right equipment, choose the correct flies, practice often, fish in the right places, and learn about the sport. When you see the graceful flick of the fly line as it darts over the fisherman's head, pauses briefly, changes direction, and then gently lights on the water, a lot of skill and practice has preceded that elegant motion. It's not automatic; it requires physical and mental abilities to combine flawlessly.

Love doesn't come to us automatically either. When we accept Jesus, He blesses us with His love. But, like fly-fishing, sharing that love contains complexities. We may feel we've just nailed down one part of loving well when we're made aware of somewhere else we've failed. Maybe we've learned to suffer long, but kindness is still difficult—we're like the fisherman who knows how to cast but chooses the wrong fly for his stream.

How do we solve our spiritual dilemma? Maybe we need to consciously practice loving. As we make it a priority to treat other people kindly and with respect, we improve. But just as we won't fly-fish well without the proper stream or lake information, we can't love without help. Unless we know God's Word and follow His Spirit's leading, we'll love clumsily, like a new fisherman who hasn't gotten it all together.

As we draw nearer to God and allow His Spirit access to our lives, the complexities lessen. While we once had to keep an eye on every element, some become more natural. We give thanks for God's work in our lives and begin to tell others of it. Suddenly we're fishing for a different species—people who need to know Jesus.

Satisfied!

*You open Your hand and satisfy
the desire of every living thing.*
PSALM 145:16 NKJV

Would God give a sparrow all it needs for life
and leave a human out of the loop? Obviously,
the Creator doesn't forget or ignore anything.
Without Him, the earth wouldn't exist. The
universe can't keep its course apart from His
command. But sometimes we wonder if we've
somehow disconnected from God. We may
seek out all kinds of odd alternatives to God,
when our desires seem to have been sidelined
and we can't see the way clearly.

All along, God never forgot our needs. The
plan hasn't changed, and He hasn't written
this verse out of scripture—even temporarily.
He knows all our questions, doubts, and
troubles and has an answer for each. But the

answers we expect and the ones He gives may be startlingly different. In part, that's because we have different outlooks. We want every desire filled by tomorrow (or at least next year), while He's viewing a longer plan. Our immediate gratification isn't His final goal—but our good is.

Look back on some things you wanted God to do, a week, a year, or several years back. Some may remain unfulfilled, but many have been accomplished. He's seen you through a lot as you've walked together. And you've been able to testify to His faithfulness as He met those needs. Continue to walk steadily with your Lord, and He'll fulfill many more desires. Then, at the end of life, you'll see that any He left behind were best done so, and you'll offer this one-word testimony: satisfied!

Salvation Satisfaction

"With long life I will satisfy him,
and show him My salvation."
PSALM 91:16 NKJV

Would you like an adventuresome life, one in which you see God do many exciting acts? How would you like to see all the wonderful things He could do in your life, in the lives of others, and in the world? Getting a front-row seat to God's wonders would be great, wouldn't it?

Well, whether you have a globe-trotting ministry or are a stay-at-home mom, God offers that to you. God plans to prove His salvation to you in many unmistakable ways. He wants to spend many years showing you all the details of His love.

That doesn't mean that every day will be exciting. We all have some dull-as-dust times when we wonder what's going on. But we'll also face enough challenges to assure us that life won't be dull. Just when we think we've got a real handle on Christianity, God can show us how little we really know of His personality and character. What had begun to seem quiet and lack challenge quickly becomes a moment-by-moment faith fight.

When we're in those exciting moments, we often wonder if our faith will stand the test. Can we hold on long enough to see the work of God in our lives and the lives of others, or will we give in? Tied up in such worries, we miss the point. God is showing His salvation. Dependence on ourselves gets us nowhere, for we cannot be faithful enough. But leaning on God, especially when we feel weakest, brings us safely through the most exciting challenge.

We're not relying on ourselves but the One who has promised us salvation. What we can't do alone, He's already done for us. Recognize that, and we're satisfied.

Good Things

I know that nothing is better for them than to rejoice, and to do good in their lives, and also that every man should eat and drink and enjoy the good of all his labor—it is the gift of God.

ECCLESIASTES 3:12–13 NKJV

When God gives you a good thing—a new house, a child, or a special job—do you hesitate to enjoy it? Do you fear paying a price because it's just "too good"? Or do you feel guilty because you have something another person doesn't have?

Where does the idea that Christians should not enjoy life come from? Not from the Bible. Perhaps it's a lie straight from hell, because scripture often speaks of the blessings God gives His people—and some are physical.

That doesn't mean enjoyment is our primary goal in life. We shouldn't mainly seek out wealth and fortune. God describes these things as fleeting, and putting our trust in them will only lead to sorrow. An "eat, drink and be merry" lifestyle (Luke 12:19) isn't appropriate for the Christian; Jesus' parable clearly shows that. When our priorities become messed up and we put possessions and pleasure before God, we can expect trouble.

But that doesn't mean we can't rejoice when God gives us worldly goods and can't make wise use of them. When we thank God for His blessings and use them properly—to help others and support our families in a responsible Christian lifestyle—those temporary things become blessings He can use through us. That's just what God intended.

If you work hard for your money and are rewarded, you can appreciate God's gift and use it for blessing. Then you'll have done right and won't be the only one who rejoices.

Fully Blessed

"And there you shall eat before the LORD your God, and you shall rejoice in all to which you have put your hand, you and your households, in which the LORD your God has blessed you."

DEUTERONOMY 12:7 NKJV

When the Israelites were ready to head into the Promised Land, God had Moses remind them of their past and His faithfulness to them. The prophet warned them not to fall into idolatry and told them God was going to give them a new place to worship. This promise follows those instructions.

God wasn't trying to make their new life hard on His people or deny them good things. Instead He planned on bringing them much joy—both through the physical blessings of good land and a fulfilled spiritual promise. Those warnings were meant to bring them only the best He had to offer.

We too have seen God turn us aside from places we want to go or things we want to do. Maybe He's denied us a desired job, the "perfect" mate, or some other good thing. When that's happened, maybe it's because it wouldn't be as wonderful as we think. What we see through rose-colored glasses, God observes clearly. And because all He wants is our good, He stops us before we get involved.

But when we put aside the things that would distract us from Him and work or worship where He wants us to, our lives are fully blessed. We can worship Him for the things He has given us—the physical and spiritual joys that leap off our tongues as we think of all our Savior has given.

Best of Both Worlds

"For this is how God loved the world:
He gave his one and only Son, so that
everyone who believes in him will not
perish but have eternal life."

John 3:16 NLT

You've known someone who looked for love in the worst places. Desperate to feel wanted, that man or woman jumped from love interest to love interest, but the results were rarely good.

But all of us could admit we desperately need love. This harsh world attacks us if we have no one to love and be loved by. Our empty hearts begin to despair when love seems to pass us by.

What many hurting people—even some Christians—fail to recognize is that human love only goes so far. Exciting romance feels good, but it doesn't solve every problem; in fact, it can be the beginning of even bigger troubles, if you're not careful. Then the hurt of love gone wrong can dry out your soul. It's not the love this world is founded on, so it can never give us all we need.

But there's one love that every person, weak or strong, can enjoy. It won't lead to a bad place or break a heart. It doesn't die out, as so many romances do, and no one feels used at the end of it. God's love is perfect, so no baggage ties it down or ruins it. Not only that, God's love never ends. He plans to bring us into eternity with Him. So the love that buoys us up today never disappears.

But link romantic love and the love of the Savior, and you have a winning combination. It's the best of both worlds!

Tongue and Heart

But those who obey God's word truly show how completely they love him. That is how we know we are living in him. Those who say they live in God should live their lives as Jesus did.

1 John 2:5–6 nlt

Want to fully experience God's perfect love? Then obey Him. Talking a good line about being a faithful Christian might seem nice, but it doesn't quite cut it. God knows His really devoted servants, and He doesn't recognize them by their mouths but by their hearts and their actions.

That doesn't mean our mouths aren't part of our obedience. The words we say are one piece of our testimony. When we speak kind words instead of harsh critiques, when we avoid saying anything that would bring God into disgrace, we use our mouths to do His will. But when we speak to bring ourselves honor instead of God, we've clearly missed the boat.

People around us won't miss the truth though. Non-Christians recognize those who mean what they say and live it out too. These believers frequently get respect for their commitment, even from others who don't agree with them. But the Christian who talks a lot about his commitment but can't stop to help a person in trouble or hesitates to help a coworker on her team clearly identifies a critical faith weakness.

When we walk the way Jesus did, like Him, we obey the Father. Instead of taking the glory for ourselves, we lift up the One who really deserves it. That's when that perfect love not only comes from our tongues but from our hearts too.

All Eternity

He has made everything beautiful in its time.
Also He has put eternity in their hearts,
except that no one can find out the work
that God does from beginning to end.

ECCLESIASTES 3:11 NKJV

Have you looked at God's stars and marveled as they lit the velvet-dark sky? Watched a sunset in which the sky is tinted from the lightest blue on the horizon to a deep tone above and delighted in God's paintbrush? Then you've seen Him make things beautiful in their time. A few hours later, those delights disappeared into the daylight, which has its own set of glories.

Though we appreciate our changing world, we only understand so much of it. Even the best scientists cannot describe every detail of our world, from its first day to the present. And if they could, they still couldn't so combine it with beauty that we could appreciate both simultaneously. God is so much greater than we can be. None of us can fully aspire to His greatness.

Though we're not up to the task of fully understanding all He does, this glorious God still wants us near Him. We can't meet Him on His own terms, yet He wants us so much that He offered us the great blessing of eternity in our hearts. Even the beauty of a magnificent world can't fill our hearts and souls. He has given us the desire to spend all eternity with Him.

So while you're gazing at that beautiful sky, don't forget to praise the One who created it and you—and be thankful that you were one He decided to share eternity with.

The Spacious Place

He brought me out into a spacious place;
he rescued me because he delighted in me.
PSALM 18:19

Have you ever wondered why God chose to save you and not your brother, sister, neighbor, or friend? Perhaps you've looked at yourself honestly and decided, if it were your choice, you might have saved another person and left yourself behind. (But how glad you feel that God decided to pour His grace out on you!) Then you start to wonder if He'll ever give the same blessing to that non-Christian.

You could wonder about these questions for a lifetime and still never have an answer. God doesn't give us the whys of His salvation. He's not required to tell us His reasons for doing anything, much less saving us. Nor does He have to tell us if He plans on saving another.

It's enough for us to know that God *did* save us, and He did it to please Himself. But that doesn't really end the matter. David's psalm, of which this is only a part, also talks about the believer's responsibility to obey God. Will that loved one hear the Good News? Perhaps only if you share it. And if the message isn't heard, there is still prayer. Few of us hear the message once and run to God. But hard hearts can still be opened with consistent prayer.

Living in the spacious place doesn't mean we want to stay there alone. We'd rather share our space with those emotionally close to us. But if they won't come, perhaps another will. As we share His news, others join us in that spacious place that never becomes crowded— there's always more room in God's love. He's always delighted to share it with another of His children.

Under Control

He covers the heavens with clouds,
provides rain for the earth, and makes
the grass grow in mountain pastures.
Psalm 147:8 nlt

We may complain when rain washes out the church picnic, but in the middle of a drought, our view changes entirely. We search the sky for clouds as our lawns or crops wither and die. As reservoir levels dip, we may even begin to pray seriously for a change of weather. When rain comes—not just drizzle but a downpour—we feel God's blessing.

How often do we see bad weather as a blessing? We're more likely to lament the game that got canceled or the snow that made our holiday visit impossible.

Let's remember that the weather is not ours to command, but God's. Unlike our daily schedules, we cannot control how much rain we get in a year or when the next storm will come. If that were left up to us, we'd probably quickly discover we're happy to leave the details to the Almighty. Keeping up with weather all over the world for even a single day would tax us beyond our powers.

Instead, we need to give thanks even for the daily blessings God offers us—rain that keeps wells and reservoirs filled, enough snow to make a white Christmas but not impede traffic, or sunshine for a special outing.

When the weather doesn't go "our way," we can still thank God that He's in control. Maybe our date wasn't more important than a growing harvest or a full water well. And when we have an overabundance of rain or snow, we can count on it that He knows what He's doing. He has it all under control.

The World or Jesus?

Anyone who wanders away from this teaching has no relationship with God. But anyone who remains in the teaching of Christ has a relationship with both the Father and the Son.

2 JOHN 9 NLT

Plenty of non-Christians denigrate Christians for their "narrowmindedness." They prefer to believe their own ideas are creative, open-minded, or freer than the teachings of Jesus. Before long, they may even have Christians wondering if their beliefs—or lack of them—are better than the "restrictive" teachings of our Lord.

Before you follow those ideas or feel as if you're hopelessly outdated, reread this passage from John's second letter. John probably received similar complaints from the Gnostics, whom you might call the New Agers of his day.

The fledgling church, standing up to wrong teachings, had a hard time of it. People didn't approve of Christianity any more then than they do now. Christians faced much opposition, and John had to remind believers just what they'd put their faith in.

Any Christian in any age can wander off into teaching that has little or nothing to do with Jesus. But will it really be better, as the non-Christian claims? John reminds Christians of the consequence of that kind of change: losing touch with Jesus. Those of us who have come to believe in Him treasure our contact with the Savior. That's why Christians spend so much time in prayer and Bible study. Would we really want to give up the intimate relationship with Him for anything a human has to offer?

The choice is simple: the world or Jesus? Will we wander to something better? No! We can't give up anything that's better than He is.

The Bitter End

"Don't call me Naomi," she responded.
"Instead, call me Mara, for the Almighty
has made life very bitter for me."
RUTH 1:20 NLT

Naomi made a pun here that gets a little lost in the translation, unless you read your Bible notes. Her name means "pleasant," but since life hadn't been very good for her for a long time, she asked her people to call her Mara, or "bitter," instead.

When a famine threatened, Naomi and her family moved out of Israel and went to Moab. After more than ten years, her husband and sons died. Naomi returned to Bethlehem with nothing but one of her daughters-in-law, Ruth. It wasn't a happy return, so when people asked, "Is this really Naomi?" she responded with the above sentences.

Like Naomi, we may have bitter days.

Everything that surrounds our lives seems unpalatable. Perhaps we see no hope for the future and could respond as she did. But like Naomi, when we feel that way, we are not looking at the end of the story. As long as we live, God is not finished writing our tale. This bitter patch may be the dark part of the story that just precedes the happiest parts of our lives. If we give up, we'll never reach the best part of the story.

When we hold on until the bitter end, like Naomi, we may find it isn't bitter at all. She found herself the center of a loving family, with a grandson to carry on the family name. Best of all, God used that infant to create something of eternal value—he became a forebear of God's Son, Jesus. Could anything that created the Light of the world remain bitter for long?

Delightful Day

He also brought me out into a broad place;
He delivered me because He delighted in me.
PSALM 18:19 NKJV

Following a blizzard touted as "the storm of the century," my bassets decided to do "snow angels" in the more-than-fourteen-inch snowbank called my front yard. Though their backs were just about even with the top of it, they bounced atop the white stuff and plowed on, leaving leg and belly marks.

I admit I laughed, though I also kept an eye on them to be sure they were safe. It was really rather fun to see them enjoying themselves and taking on a new challenge. They'd never seen this much snow.

Somewhat like a pet owner who gets a lot of enjoyment from the animal's antics, I imagine God delights in watching us take on new things, enjoy the world He's created for us, and learn more of Him. He didn't create us to become our taskmaster but because He wanted to share things with us not only in eternity but here on earth too. Though scripture contains many serious warnings and guidelines, there are frequent indications of the joy He has in His creation, and part of that creation is us.

So while we're trying to do the right thing and follow His way intently, let's not forget that we can also simply rejoice in the God who saved us. He delivered us because He delighted in us, and He wants us to delight in Him too.

Make this a truly delightful day as you worship the Savior who loves you in so many ways. Remember, He wants to share the fun with you as well.

Redirection

For whom the LςRD loves He corrects,
just as a father the son in whom he delights.
PROVERBS 3:12 NKJV

In today's "independent" society, the idea of correcting your child isn't popular. So much so that a parent with a disruptive child often hesitates to do anything in public beyond a weak "Johnny, stop that." To do more might court criticism or even the risk of losing the child altogether.

But God denies the current child-raising theory that hesitates to redirect a child with firmness. He says a loving parent will correct the child properly—with love and kindness and with enough firmness to make it stick. Not to do that would be to ignore the child's best interests.

We've experienced that kind of correction

in our own spiritual lives; and though we may have doubted it was a blessing when we first felt it, as we've grown in Christ, we've learned how right this verse is. God bothers to tell us when we've done wrong or missed His path because He cares where we end up. Though we initially find the correction unpleasant, in the end we learn it's because He wants us to experience the best life possible. We can only know we've done wrong when He helps us see the better way we should have gone.

The kind of independence that ignores God's correction costs us heavily. We've seen it in those who reject Him entirely or who claim to accept Christ but never walk in His way. Do we really want to live that way, or will we take the course correction our Savior has to offer?

Honey to the Soul

*Kind words are like honey—sweet to
the soul and healthy for the body.*
PROVERBS 16:24 NLT

One of the great blessings of the Christian life is
a kind word spoken just when you need to hear
it. One thing that should set Christians apart
from unbelievers is consistent, caring kindness.
When you don't find kindness in the church,
something has gone wrong. A critical spirit isn't
from God and can't help the soul and body.

But we also can't expect the church to always
agree with everything we do. When we've fallen
into wrongdoing, it is the responsibility of caring
Christians to confront us lovingly and set us
on the right track. When we respond to that
correction, we can again feel the kindness of
those who have loved us well enough to tell
us we've been wrong. We might have missed it

when we were doing wrong, but wise Christians will still have used it to draw us back to the right path.

People have a hard time hearing critics, unless they know care is also there. A combination of correction and kindness often makes the difference in whether those words are really heard. Honey spreads easily on the soul, while criticism feels like sand in an open wound.

Whether you need to encourage or redirect another Christian, are you speaking kind words? If so, their sweetness may bring just the healing God has in mind.

Sweet Words

How sweet your words taste to me;
they are sweeter than honey.
PSALM 119:103 NLT

When you're looking for some sweetness in a sour life, turn to scripture. Read the story of Joseph, who triumphed over his brothers' jealousy and slavery. Discover how brave Esther saved her people. Follow the soul-saving story of Jesus' ministry. Read Psalms for encouragement from a king.

As you read, feel blessed. Non-Christians don't get this feeling about scripture. To them, without the Holy Spirit's prompting, the Bible remains a closed book. Some read it but come away with wrong ideas about it. Others never seem to get beyond a few pages.

But the scriptures are God's huge love letter to His own people. As even the newest believer reads attentively, His mercy becomes clear. Yet a lifelong believer can read the same passage and see something new again and again. God's relationship with the Christian constantly grows through His Book, and with it, He shows new depth at every stage of growth.

Don't get caught up in the mysteries of scripture and miss the plain, blessed truth of how much God loves you today. Over and over, in many ways, He's made it clear that He cared enough to die for you. Rather than enjoying heaven with only the angels, it was important to Him to share it with humans too. All He asks is that you believe in His Son.

He's left you the story of Jesus in His Book, but that's not all He offers. He wants His Spirit to help you understand and make those words sweet. Have you read those words and felt the sweetness of His heart?

One Great Day

Every tongue will confess that Jesus Christ is Lord, to the glory of God the Father.
PHILIPPIANS 2:11 NASB

Someday, Jesus' greatness will be unavoidable. Even the deepest doubters and those who lived in a fashion entirely contradictory to His teachings will have to admit He rules heaven and earth. It will be a hard day for unbelievers. Imagine their having to admit very publicly that they've been so wrong. Not only will they have to accept their huge mistake, but they must bow down to the Jesus whom they so misjudged. Their stiff knees will finally bend before the Lord of heaven and earth (Philippians 2:10).

But on that great day, what joy faithful followers will feel! In one moment, all the truths we've put faith in will become concrete before us. Instead of simply trusting, we'll have perfect proof that our faith was right. Before our eyes will be all the things we have understood spiritually for so very long.

Where the doubters feel agony, we will experience the purest pleasure. Giving Jesus the glory on that day will be our greatest delight—one we look forward to with anticipation even now.

We yearn for that glorious day, but until it comes, the work Jesus gave us is not yet done. Faith, lived out consistently, may turn some doubting hearts to the Savior. Then instead of being horrified by their wrong judgment, they too will share the blessing of praise for Jesus.

We who once deserved condemnation have seen it turned aside for mercy—fulfilling the message our Savior had all along. Let's share that with as many as we can.

Faithful Testimony

Now Stephen, a man full of God's grace and power, performed great wonders and signs among the people. Opposition arose, however.
ACTS 6:8–9

It's not uncommon when you're doing a work for God's kingdom to face opposition. Just when a ministry is beginning to bear fruit or when you're helping others greatly, little things may cause disruptions or larger issues may bring it to a halt.

Instead of giving yourself over to the frustration, recognize that even very prominent Christians have suffered similar problems. It's not uncommon for nonbelievers to become jealous of a good work. Like Stephen, you may have run aground on someone else's attitude. But whatever the problem, if you've been faithful, you are on the right track and God will stand firm with you.

The new deacon's problems didn't come from his own weakness or lack of faith. Scripture makes it clear Stephen gave a powerful witness to God's work. His testimony to the Sanhedrin was a model sermon—it just wasn't popular with people who didn't want to hear the truth.

When troubles come against us, as they did against Stephen, we can follow his example and continue to bear God's witness. Because the deacon opened his mouth, despite the danger, God gave him a potent testimony. Even as his opponents stoned him, Stephen spoke of the power of faith in Jesus.

Chances might be slim we would lose our lives for our faith, but we may fear loss of work, family, or popularity. The God who remained faithful to Stephen also supports us. If we stand firm, no matter what the outcome, like that first-century deacon, we will effectively lift up His name.

Fully Joyous

"I have told you this so that you will be filled with my joy. Yes, your cup of joy will overflow!"
JOHN 15:11 TLB

Overflowing joy! We tend to connect that with a feeling of freedom. When a wonderful, unusual event occurs or when we are released from a burden of fear, this is the way we respond.

Do we also associate joy with obedience to God? Maybe not as often. Yet the "this" Jesus talked about in the above verse was the obedience that caused the disciples to remain in His love. You can't separate Christian love, obedience, and joy. They work together to describe God's kingdom to us.

As long as we set our ideas above God's and don't take His commands seriously enough to obey them, we won't feel the intense joy of knowing Him deeply. Separation occurs because we will not submit to Him. We've tacitly said we don't believe God knows what He's talking about in His Word. And He takes that very personally.

As long as we intentionally disobey God, we cannot experience full joy. But those who seek to do His will, though they don't achieve it perfectly, experience an increasingly profound relationship with Him. God knows our weaknesses and does not require perfection before He communes with us. But He desires that we commit ourselves to Him and follow His Word. When we consistently walk with Him, He connects with us and aids us in living out His Word. The more we live for Him, the more our joy communicates itself to the world, just as God ordained.

Finally, in heaven, we'll become completely joyous as we meet with the God we have trusted so long. As our delight in our Redeemer pours from us, we'll sing His praises eternally.

Lightened Burdens

"Come to Me, all you who labor and are heavy laden, and I will give you rest."
MATTHEW 11:28 NKJV

After a long, frustrating day at work, we all know what it is to crave rest. Whether we use our muscles or brains on the job, we know what it is to be worn out.

But people wear out spiritually too. When we don't make it to church for a couple of weeks, even if we had good reasons why we couldn't make it, the wear and tear on our spirits can begin to show. Or perhaps we've been faithful in a ministry, but it hasn't left us much time to relax, and our bodies are beginning to tell us we've overdone it.

We need to use some sense when we're tired. Maybe what we really need is help so we can make it to church—a ride from a friend or help with whatever keeps us away—or a little extra rest. But we shouldn't stop at the sensible things, because we could rest all week and still feel heavily burdened. Extra sleep or relaxation can only do so much, though they're a good place to start.

Jesus also tells us to come to Him when weariness floods our souls. We can do that many ways. More time than usual in prayer and personal Bible study may help. Or perhaps we can benefit from listening to a special Christian speaker or reading an encouraging book. Whatever we need for refreshment and wherever we turn, our focus needs to be on God. When we drink deeply at His well, the energy will begin to flow.

Then our burdens will become light, and we'll be ready for work again.

In the Shepherd's Arms

He will feed His flock like a shepherd;
He will gather the lambs with His arm,
and carry them in His bosom, and gently
lead those who are with young.

ISAIAH 40:11 NKJV

We may not appreciate being compared to sheep. We like to think of ourselves as sophisticated, admirable individuals, not such silly, often-dirty animals. But God's comparison isn't really unfair. We, like sheep, foolishly allow distractions to draw us from His care. No matter how we try, daily sin begrimes us.

Despite our messy state, when we call out in need, our Savior lifts us up and carries us in His arms or gently directs us when we're at our weakest. His soft heart cares for us, even when we aren't especially sophisticated or admirable. As Jesus' arms wrap around us,

His warm compassion floods our souls. When His children feel pain, God's comfort is so profoundly tender that nothing equals it. No one heals hearts like Jesus. Human empathy can't reach the places His Spirit entwines and soothes.

The same powerful God who rules the universe, corrects His erring children, and judges the wicked is also intensely kind to those He loves. Though wrongdoers rightly fear Him, His children need never doubt His gracious heart. He has given us a place in His love, and nothing can separate us from it.

No matter how smelly and foolish we've become, when we call on Jesus, He gathers us up, dirt and all. Cuddled in His arms, no harm comes to us. If He leads us down a path, we need not fear attack.

All that matters is that we're with Him again and never want to be apart.

Heavenly Bargain

"But lay up for yourselves treasures in heaven, where neither moth nor rust destroys and where thieves do not break in and steal."

MATTHEW 6:20 NKJV

Imagine, you can start a heavenly treasure chest while you're still here on earth! But you can't fill it with dollars, pounds, or pesos. Though no earthly currency transports to heaven, even the poorest person on earth can lay aside eternal blessings. That's because heavenly treasures have nothing to do with our legal tender— no government creates or backs it. God's riches can't be exchanged on paper or metal. They're collected in a currency of the heart that consists of things like forgiveness, humility, and charitable deeds.

Forgive a neighbor who did you wrong, and you're the one who pays the price, yet you do not lose whatever you gave. God stores it up in His eternal memory, and when you reach heaven, you'll find an even greater value placed upon your response than could have been given on earth. Not only that, the benefit doesn't last only for as long as your neighbor lives next to you, but forever!

On top of that, any good thing you do because you love Jesus won't disappear. Thieves can't remove it from you, the government can't tax you on it, and fire won't burn it down. Nothing can destroy it or take the shine from it.

When you think about it, even if you have plenty of cash, do you want to use it to buy a few extra clothes or support God's kingdom? Are you putting your money into moth food or feeding a person's soul? One lasts a few years and the other for eternity. Which is the better bargain?

Brimming with His Spirit

May God give you more and
more mercy, peace, and love.
JUDE 2 NLT

What a blessing to continually receive more and
more of God's mercy, peace, and love. That's just
the kind of Christian life we'd like to have—
until we're bursting with these good spiritual
experiences to the point where we simply can't
hold them in.

Maybe we have already received so much
from God. Our lives have changed drastically
because of the salvation He offered. But
bursting? Perhaps we wouldn't use that word
to describe ourselves.

That's because God doesn't overfill us with
His blessings. He gives us enough to share
then waits to see what we do with them. Like
a good steward, He's not going to splurge with

blessings then watch them sit being ignored or only used for personal gain. God gives blessings so we can encourage, teach, and lead others into a relationship with Him. He doesn't give them so that we can bulge with His unused gifts.

But if we receive God's gifts and pass them on to others, take hold of His Word and teachings, and use them to show others how to live, God fills us again. The concept isn't for us to become spiritual gluttons but for us to be filled, share those benefits, and, as we empty, to allow His Spirit to make us full again.

When we've made that our lifestyle, we are truly blessed—and so are others who come in contact with us. Their growth in turn touches others' lives—and on and on it goes. The joys of mercy, peace, and love abound, just as God planned.

Glad Worship

I was glad when they said unto me,
Let us go into the house of the LORD.
PSALM 122:1 KJV

Have you had one of those Sundays when just getting to church was a challenge? Maybe one of your children was sick on Saturday night, and you stayed up too late. Or you got together with friends, and the fellowship was so good you lost track of time; then when you got to bed, it was simply too late. Or maybe you're having a challenge with another church member and just don't look forward to seeing that person.

Rolling out of bed in the morning may not be your favorite thing, but don't let that keep you from getting together with your congregation for worship. Don't make a habit of not getting there on time, because even if you're tired, you will miss out on a lot of joy. Avoid church more than once, and you'll probably begin to feel empty or as if you've lost something.

God puts gladness in the human heart at the thought of worshipping Him in the company of other believers. It's a kind of sharing you won't find in the office, with your non-Christian friends, or in a social club. Only a fellowship of believers who share love for God feels the joy David describes here.

If things aren't perfect at your church or you're having a disagreement with someone, don't let it keep you from God's house. After all, you're there to worship Him, not that person. As an added benefit, He might even help you settle your differences peacefully.

Gifts for Eternity

*The generous will prosper; those who refresh
others will themselves be refreshed.*

PROVERBS 11:25 NLT

God offers Christians this wonderful blessing:
those who give will also receive. Whether it's
money, time, energy, or another commodity,
spiritual or physical, God does not forget
anything we've done. Just like the gift of a
cup of cold water that He will see gets its just
reward (Matthew 10:42), God never ignores any
generous gifts we offer at a price to ourselves.

In a world that tries to hoard time, money,
and love, Jesus calls us to do just the opposite.
We are to care for those who hurt, lift up
those who can't help themselves, and look out
for our brothers and sisters. As we do that, we
don't lose out, as unbelievers expect. Instead
our lives are mysteriously revived and refilled.

Loss is the final reward of those who fear to give. They hold on to their money, but they never have enough, while a generous neighbor prospers, even if she doesn't have a lot of free cash. Others cling tightly to their love, rarely sharing it, only to have it slip out of their hands.

Whether or not a person is a Christian, this truth works in each life. Generous unbelievers may benefit from it—at least in this world. Christians who do not learn generosity may enter eternity with little to show for their time on earth.

Want refreshment? Do not hold too tightly to the things God loans you for a few decades on earth. Giving allows you to receive not only here but for eternity.

Whole Cure

He fell to the ground at Jesus' feet,
thanking him for what he had done.
This man was a Samaritan.
LUKE 17:16 NLT

Jesus healed ten lepers, but only the Samaritan had a tender enough conscience to come back and give thanks. Though the Jews considered his race outcasts, this "unacceptable" man showed a spirit nine of their own people lacked. As we read the story, we begin to wonder: *Why did the other nine fail to come? Had they not received an equal blessing? Did they think they "deserved" what they got?*

Leprosy was a terrible, incurable disease in the first century. To have it meant spending your life as an outcast so you wouldn't pass it on to others. But the nine didn't connect the comparison between their physical and spiritual conditions. Obviously, this man understood that once he'd been separated from God, and now he had relationship with the Holy One. Not to thank Him would have been unconscionable.

Jesus promised the man his faith had healed him. What of the other nine? Whatever happened to their bodies, their souls certainly lacked closeness to the Savior. All they could pass on to others was information about their brief, seemingly joyless, contact with Jesus.

But the healed man had something other than disease to talk about. He received the body and soul healing only Jesus offers. His faith, the Savior promised, made him whole. Instead of disease, his life, even in this one recorded act, shared the joy of knowing Jesus.

Are we trying to share a joyless faith that's worse than leprosy, or have we experienced the whole healing of Jesus? If our souls have not rejoiced in the Good News, we need to return to the only One who has the cure.

Blessed Peace

*"God blesses those who work for peace,
for they will be called the children of God."*
MATTHEW 5:9 NLT

When we think of peace, it's often in connection
with an international peace process. But here
Jesus isn't only speaking to world leaders.
God's peace has a much larger picture, one
every Christian takes part in. By bringing the
message of the Good News to others, we offer
lasting peace to the human heart.

Many churches address this need in many
ways. They start by bringing the Gospel message
to hurting people but don't stop there. After
people come to know Jesus, they have not
exhausted God's peace. Battles may still rage
in their homes. That's why many churches
continue bringing peace to struggling families
by offering weekend studies or Bible classes that

help couples have a better marriage or parents relate better to their children.

God doesn't put a "peace" stamp on our lives the day we commit ourselves to Him. Though our lives improve with that choice, no automatic alteration impacts our families. This verse is right when it says peace—whether between nations or individuals—is work.

But we need not worry. When God gives us a task, He also empowers us to accomplish it. He blesses our efforts, though they may not bear fruit immediately. Even when others ignore our attempts, obedience changes our own lives and improves our Christian walks. We draw closer to God, even if we cannot improve the lives of others.

God doesn't command that we be successful in our peacemaking, though we may be. He only requires us to work at it. Blessings for that obedience will still come from His hand.

Morning Joy

For His anger is but for a moment,
His favor is for life; weeping may endure
for a night, but joy comes in the morning.
PSALM 30:5 NKJV

When God redirects a life, it often causes pain. We humans don't enjoy being told we've headed off in the wrong direction. And if God's redirection means we have to change a habit, we may experience trouble redesigning our lives. We may even ask ourselves if God still loves us.

God reminds us that His anger at sin is only short term. Like a loving parent, He plans to deal with the problem and move on in love. Correction doesn't last as long as blessing. And though we may resist leaving our wrongdoing behind, He insists on it because He's looking out for our long-term good.

We have a choice—we can keep going our

own way or accept the changes God wants to make in our lives. Or to put it another way, we can stay stuck in our own unprofitable spot or learn a new way that will bring us blessings.

Though we may suffer for a short time, as we submit to God instead of resisting His Spirit, we receive joy and a new lifestyle that benefits us for years—and eternity. Whether the suffering lasts for one dark night as we agonize over a simple problem or clings for years, we can be certain joy will follow. Even if we never see the greatest benefit on earth, we can count on rejoicing in eternity. In that forever morning, we'll praise the Father who gave brief pain but everlasting joy.

Success Principles

"Study this Book of Instruction continually. Meditate on it day and night so you will be sure to obey everything written in it. Only then will you prosper and succeed in all you do."

Joshua 1:8 NLT

Many businesspeople attribute their success to the truths they've learned in the Bible. And if you run a business by following scriptural truths, you may well lead effectively. But when this verse talks about prosperity and success, it's not simply referring to financial or business success. Joshua wasn't really concerned about either. But he did have a mission—to bring God's people into the Promised Land.

Once they got there, the people could choose to live as God commanded or take their beautiful surroundings for granted. If they remembered their past and lived by the law Moses brought to them, God would make them successful—their harvests would overflow. But how much grain they raised or how many animals filled their fields was not the best prosperity the Israelites could have. It might come as the result of an intimate relationship with God, but it couldn't replace that fellowship.

You've seen people with millions—or even billions—of dollars who have material prosperity but don't seem happy. They can buy everything they want, but they don't relate well to a spouse or raise happy children. But some people who barely cover their expenses have the same problems.

The answer, no matter how much cash you have, remains the same. Truly successful relationships are based on God. Those who know the Word, follow God faithfully, and live what He has taught them won't have perfect lives, but they can develop increasingly better ones as they follow the guidelines of the Master.

Unchangeable

"*I am the Lord, and I do not change.
That is why you descendants of Jacob
are not already destroyed.*"
MALACHI 3:6 NLT

Listen to any two pollsters' results, and you'll
begin to wonder if people either don't know
what they believe or don't tell the truth about
it twice in a row. But in fact, people have very
changeable minds. Media coverage may influence
them, or a friend may speak persuasively and
alter the direction of their thinking. Or they
may be confused about an issue.

None of that is true of our Creator. Only
God doesn't change His opinion and always
knows what to think. When He says something, He means it.

That's good, because with the disobedience He's had from humans—both Jacob's

descendants, whom Malachi spoke to, and today's believers—changing His mind might seem like a good idea. If He'd been a more mutable God, He might have immediately given up on people instead of sending Jesus to save us.

Though we may feel tempted to ignore this verse because it talks about destruction, or we may want to object because it seems like a threat from God, it's neither of those things. Actually, this is a positive statement. God reminds us that He could have destroyed us all because we sin. We're guilty as charged. None of us has never disobeyed God. Even after we accept His grace, our struggle with sin remains. So when God explains that He could have changed but didn't, it's reason to rejoice.

We should praise God because He doesn't need a pollster to make a choice and isn't influenced even by the best arguments or our worst actions. God is faithful to Himself and does not change. Let's rejoice.

Daddy God

*And because you are sons, God has sent
forth the Spirit of His Son into your
hearts, crying out, "Abba, Father!"*
GALATIANS 4:6 NKJV

You are God's child. Consider that carefully and
feel the amazement of that truth.

The Creator of the universe, the all-powerful
God, who didn't even begin to wear Himself
out making our world, much less the universe,
wants to be your Daddy (after all, that's what
Abba means). This awesome being wants you to
come to Him as a young child who trusts Him
and seeks His love and protection.

Nothing that happens is beyond the Lord's
domain. Nothing can touch us that the heavenly
Father can't deal with, and no event can ruin
His plan for good in our lives. All things, He
promises, will work together for our good if we

love Him (Romans 8:28).

God didn't simply have the prophets write down the Bible and leave us to figure out His love for ourselves. He actually put part of Himself in our hearts when we accepted the sacrifice of His Son—the Spirit entered us in a moment, and He hasn't left since, even when we've ignored Him and denied His work in our lives.

Like a daddy, God never gives up on us, even in our disobedience. But just because He did forgive, we can't take advantage by forgetting He is still Lord of the universe and treating Him without respect. Because He loved us, He did not hold the sin against us, but our Lord is no wimp. He disciplines unrepentant children. If He didn't do that, He wouldn't be our Daddy.

Heavenly Places

*But God, who is rich in mercy. . .raised us
up together, and made us sit together in
the heavenly places in Christ Jesus.*
EPHESIANS 2:4, 6 NKJV

A heavenly place awaits every Christian, a spot
in heaven with Jesus where we can experience
every good thing in the eternal joy of the Father.

When we talk about being in glory with
Jesus, do we take it lightly? Do we assume we're
going to be there because we somehow deserve
it? Hardly. On our own, we'd never reach heaven.
Even if we filled our lives with good works, we'd
never become holy. Only God can make that
change in our lives when we trust in the work
of His Son, Jesus.

But God, in His mercy, offers us the ability
to spend eternity with Him, not in a little hole
of a place or in the worst corner of His kingdom

or down the street from the best place in town. Instead He gives us the prime spot, with His Son, Jesus.

Knowing the blessing that lies before us should humble our hearts. Because we know our eternal, royal destiny, we must follow our Savior's path and seek to show all those who have never received mercy the rich blessings that lie before them if they accept the sacrifice of God's only begotten Son.

No spot in eternity exists for those who assume they are better than others, because God graciously offered them this gift. The Father offers no room to the proud and disdainful. So let's start living today as we plan to spend our eternity as children of the merciful King. He gave us life in heavenly places; can we do any less than model that joyful message?

Driving Wind

*"But suddenly, your ruthless enemies
will be crushed like the finest of dust.
Your many attackers will be driven
away like chaff before the wind."*
ISAIAH 29:5 NLT

All sorts of dangerous enemies on the horizon
strike fear into our hearts. Whether it's a person
we'd rather not face, the loss of a loved one, or a
lifelong problem, we'd like to see them suddenly
disappear. Like chaff being tossed up into the
air by a farmer and disappearing from his crop,
we'd like to believe they'll depart from our lives.

God promised to remove Jerusalem's
enemies this way. One day, far in the future,
their adversaries would become nothing more
than debris driven on the wind. But first, God
planned to bring His disobedient people low.
When they reached the edge of death and

recognized their neediness, He promised to come in like a driving wind and clean all the confusion from their lives.

If we're in situations that feel like spiritual or physical death and need that driving wind, God offers us a similar help. But the blessing will not come to those who have their own proud plan or solution to the problem. When our faces are in the dust, and we recognize no other God than the Lord, He answers our need, whether it's with wind, an army, or simply a touch of love.

No enemy stands before God. So if we're still facing a problem, we have to ask why. Are we standing in our own pride, or is it something God is leading us through for our own benefit?

But when God commands our enemies to depart, they'll be gone in a moment, and no one will find them floating on the wind. Then our thanks will reach up to God as we praise His works again.

Guarded by God

*But the Lord is faithful, who will establish
you and guard you from the evil one.*
2 THESSALONIANS 3:3 NKJV

Many years ago, I went on a job interview. The
position looked good and I was called in for a
second interview, but someone else ended up
getting the position. For a while, I wondered
what had happened. What had I done wrong?

Later, I realized that maybe I hadn't done
anything wrong—maybe what I had been was
"wrong." Naively, I hadn't realized that as a
Christian, I would have had conflicts with the
kind of books I'd be working with. Daily I would
have had to read things that went counter to my
faith. Instead of denying me a good thing, God
had been protecting me from something really
wrong. He was guarding me from the evil one.
Finally, I was glad I hadn't gotten what once

seemed like a wonderful spot.

God faithfully looks out for us, even when we aren't aware of problems. Instead of letting us innocently fall into trouble, He goes before us and paves the way to our making the right decision, as long as we're honestly trying to follow His will.

You've probably seen the same kind of thing in your life. Maybe there was a person you thought you wanted to marry but didn't, and later you discovered something that made you realize why God didn't let it happen. Or maybe the move you wanted to make stalled out, and when you found out why, that delay made you happy.

God looks ahead for you and establishes you in His blessings. As long as you follow His will and ask to walk in His way, you won't go wrong.

The Word's Worth

*All Scripture is given by inspiration of God,
and is profitable for doctrine, for reproof,
for correction, for instruction in righteousness,
that the man of God may be complete,
thoroughly equipped for every good work.*
2 TIMOTHY 3:16–17 NKJV

Most nonbelievers run life by their own rules. That's a recipe for disaster, since it leads to mistakes, wrong ideas, and troubles. But because they don't have a life direction, it's the best they can do. The Bible condemns this attitude when it talks about people doing what is right in their own eyes. Proverbs 12:15 describes such a person as a fool, and Psalm 14:1 defines a fool as one who does not believe in God.

But God won't leave the Christian at such a loss. He wants His people to know where they are going and be able to turn aside from wrong.

Therefore, He gave us extensive directions that show us right from wrong and how we can best serve Him and live in an upright way. When we're focused on these truths, He says we're complete to do good works.

But God also leaves it up to us. We can read His Word, or we can ignore it. He won't strong-arm us to pick up a Bible or follow what we read there. He'd rather have willing followers who have experienced the joy of knowing Him and walking in His way.

But making use of all God has offered us, learning about Him, and putting His Word into action will never lead to disaster. Though trials and troubles come, they turn to good in His hands. Who could run his or her own life that way, without the Word?

Second-Half Blessing

So the LORD blessed Job in the second half
of his life even more than in the beginning.
JOB 42:12 NLT

Our youth-loving society praises those with few years and great beauty. But it ignores what Victorian Robert Browning called "the last of life for which the first was made." About a hundred years after Browning lived, we try to avoid thoughts of life after forty. Surely the first half of life is the most blessed, we tend to believe.

For Job—and many others—that is not true. Job wrestled with his loss of home, family, and friends in the first half of life but saw incredible blessing after he'd overcome through God's grace. Though he surely mourned those lost children long afterward, he could not complain over lost herds or goods. God gave him even more once he knew Him more intimately. And though the children could never be replaced, God gave him sons and daughters again. According to scripture, his later days were even better than the first.

When the world tempts us to feel life has passed us by, let's remember we aren't finished yet. God may give us many wonderful relationships, increased spiritual growth, and physical blessings in the years ahead. Until our very last day on earth, the Savior is not done giving us good things. As long as He has a purpose for us here, He supports us in many ways.

So instead of feeling sorry for ourselves or toting up the days, months, weeks, and years that are already past, let's praise Him for all the benefits He's already given and look forward to all those that may lie ahead. As Browning also said, "The best is yet to be."

Praise Party

*We wait for the blessed hope—
the appearing of the glory of our
great God and Savior, Jesus Christ.*

TITUS 2:13

If you had to describe your greatest hope in the Christian life, what would it be? Salvation and life with Jesus in eternity? The hope that God will deal with a problem you face with a loved one? There is one greater hope, and God offers it to all His people.

One day, unexpectedly, Jesus will return. Then all who have trusted Him with their earthly lives will rejoice as they see their faith fulfilled. As our heavenly future appears before us, we will delight in God's faithfulness and begin to receive the reward He promised—to be forever with Him.

Even now, when we think of that day, our

hearts lift up in response. Hope and expectation build in our hearts as we desire Him to complete the work He's begun. Excitement for the coming of Jesus is a Christian's hopeful prerogative.

But that great, overwhelming joy won't be for everyone. When Jesus appears, no unbeliever will see a humble carpenter, but all will recognize the glorious King. No one will push Him aside. Suddenly your coworker who made fun of your faith will realize you weren't the one on the wrong track. Those who refused your testimony will understand why you persisted in telling them about Jesus.

When life seems hard and our testimonies fall on hard hearts, may the hope of Jesus never leave us. Because the prospect He offers isn't only for eternity. Today, He softens hard hearts and opens lives to their need for His love. One day, as He appears, that soul we labored to win may lift up His name in praise.

Help in Need

*For I can do everything through
Christ, who gives me strength.*

PHILIPPIANS 4:13 NLT

Is there something you could do that God would
refuse to help you with? No, not as long as
you're tapped into Him and seeking to obey His
will. Of course, that doesn't mean He'll assist
you in sin. This verse isn't the blanket statement
some folks would like to think it is.

Even for faithful Christians, this statement
isn't simply a "do as you please" one. Read the
context of this passage, and you'll see Paul is
talking about the way God helped him through
financial difficulties. The Philippians came to
his aid when no one else would, and the apostle
appreciated it. Though he'd steeled himself to
live with nothing but the barest necessities,
God's method of providing for him, by the

generous act of these believers, made that a thing of the past. God's ways were even better than Paul expected.

God will also give us more than we expect. When no one wants to help, He'll keep us on course with His task for us, even when it's hard. But as we faithfully respond to Him, He may provide unexpected blessings for us that amaze us. Like Paul, we may find ourselves saying, "You didn't have to, but I sure do appreciate it."

God's help often comes through others. Like Paul, let's not forget to give a thank-you to a faithful supporter. God helped us do all with His support, even if it came from another Christian.

Peace in Prayer

*Be anxious for nothing, but in everything by
prayer and supplication, with thanksgiving,
let your requests be made known to God.*
PHILIPPIANS 4:6 NKJV

God doesn't want us to worry or get stressed
out. So He offers a solution to those states of
mind: prayer. Nothing in this world is beyond
His control, He reminds us—there's nothing
He won't be happy to help us with, if only we
mention it to Him.

So why stick to our own worrywart
tendencies or attempt to find other ways around
the problem? Maybe we think we don't need to
bother God with something "this small." He'd
be glad to help with anything, even the tiniest
problem. Nothing is below the notice of Him
who created subatomic particles. Or maybe
we figure we don't need help on this one. He'll

be there to share the good things, and if an unexpected trouble comes up, He'll be happy to assist us too.

God is trying to tell us He wants to be a part of every moment of our lives. Whether it's something we simply need to mention or a deep concern we petition for a long time, He's interested.

Only when we give Him all our anxieties can He have the kind of impact on our lives—and on the lives of others to whom we minister—He's always had in mind. Then we'll also experience two unexpected benefits: thanksgiving and peace. We'll appreciate what our Savior begins to give and offer Him thanks, deepening and expanding our trust relationship. As we do that, harmony will fill our lives.

Find peace in prayer today.

Promise Fulfilled

*And the peace of God, which surpasses
all understanding, will guard your hearts
and minds through Christ Jesus.*

PHILIPPIANS 4:7 NKJV

If God gives peace, why don't all Christians experience it? Does He save it for some and deny it to others?

No, God offers peace to all His children. But to understand this verse, you can't take it out of context. The verse before this told us not to be anxious but to bring all our concerns to God in prayer. Prayer builds a relationship with the Savior, and the knowledge that God is in control of any trouble in our lives fosters peace in our hearts.

When you see a Christian who lacks peace, though, don't jump to judgment. Maybe the struggle he's dealing with is difficult, and he's given it to God but hasn't seen the results yet. The challenge before him is new, and he's praying hard but struggles with faith. Come alongside such a brother and encourage him that God will see him through. Or maybe she's living on a small paycheck and fears her children will lack something because she can't provide. Remind her that all provision comes from God, who has not given up on her, even if she hasn't seen it yet.

If you have years of faithful service to God at your back, you've been through such challenges and have seen the loyalty of your Savior. You can testify to another that His peace will come, and the promises will be fulfilled. So share that with struggling Christians who have committed their lives to Him but cannot see what He will do. Tell them God's faithfulness is not just for you but for all who stand firm. Then pray for that standing-firm believer and watch that fulfilled promise appear.

Stainless

"Come now, and let us reason together," says the
LORD, "Though your sins are like scarlet, they
shall be as white as snow; though they are red
like crimson, they shall be as wool."
ISAIAH 1:18 NKJV

Anyone who runs a household can tell you
how hard stains are to remove from clothing,
pots and pans, or a carpet. Unless you use the
right cleanser, a stain can remain for the rest of
that object's life or may even cause you to throw
it away. Stains can be serious business.

Household objects aren't the only things
with stains, the Bible tells us. We have one that's
hard to remove too: sin. We may have tried to
get it out by focusing on good works, but our
best efforts have proved less than successful. It's
like taking a deep, dried-in stain and running
water on it—it might move it around a bit, but

it's unlikely to eradicate the blot.

We may shove our stain around a bit—often expanding it with our good intentions to improve ourselves—but we can't escape it entirely. Sin removal is beyond the ability of any mere human. We can't perform a "sin-ectomy."

But God can get rid of sin. He covers our scarlet sins with the even deeper red of His Son's blood. Miraculously, they turn pure white, like dark ground covered with new snowfall. Where once we could only see the scars of sin, healing begins. Our aching hearts are covered with the cool, healing touch of a Savior whose balm reaches the deepest soul places.

The change has begun. In eternity we'll see what God now sees—ourselves entirely cleansed by the Son, who made us stainless with His sacrifice.

Unfailing Care

*His compassions fail not. They are new
every morning; great is Your faithfulness.*
LAMENTATIONS 3:22–23 NKJV

When trouble hits, people often start asking questions. *Where is God?* they wonder when a family member becomes seriously ill or a war starts.

It's normal to feel confusion for a while when you're hit with large problems. Getting it together mentally may take a bit of thinking and praying. But as you enter that time of confusion, be sure of one thing: God has not deserted you. As you wake to a new day of doubt and questioning, His new compassions are ready to meet you. They cannot disappear or fail you, because He promised they will be there, and for that not to be true would mean that God became faithless.

God's faithful nature never changes—if it did, He would not be the Immutable One. Imagine if God did vary: He would have given the Bible then changed His mind about what He said. Then we'd have to have multiple revisions, based on new revelations. What confusion that would lead to, because we'd never know whom to believe. Every person who claimed to have a new view of God could be right.

But God doesn't alter. What He was when the prophet Jeremiah wrote down these words is what He still is. Not a word of scripture has changed since He first inspired it—the story of His faithfulness remains the same from age to age. He has been there for all believers through the ages.

If we don't see His compassions, perhaps we've been blinded by our situation. But no event on earth changes His tender care for us. All we need is trusting faith that He will never fail. And He won't.

Brave Love

*The Lord will not cast off forever.
Though He causes grief, yet He will show
compassion according to the multitude of
His mercies. For He does not afflict willingly,
nor grieve the children of men.*
<small>LAMENTATIONS 3:31–33 NKJV</small>

Have you ever thought that God is much braver than we are at allowing His children to face trouble? We try to keep our children from as many problems as possible. Some even overprotect thoroughly rebellious children by defending them from challenges that could cause growth.

In order to get the attention of a disobedient Christian, God does not hesitate to bring a measure of hurt into that life. For a while He allows the defiant one to experience the well-earned fruits of disobedience. But He'll not allow grief to last forever. Eventually, as the wayward Christian turns and realizes the loss of God's intimate love, the Savior's multitude of mercies pour out again. Though He bravely allows His child to experience pain, it is only for a time.

Do you know someone who has walked away from God and struggles with the results of that choice? Recognize that God has not ended His love. Unlike many people, He has not written that soul off as impossible to reclaim. But also, do not take too lightly the fact that this suffering is caused by sin. Don't excuse it when you see it or tell that believer that wrongdoing has nothing to do with life's troubles.

Yet God's blessings are available to even the most disobedient child who turns from sin. Pray for that loved one to turn again and accept the Savior's love. Over and over again God gave that blessing to Israel and Judah. He'll give it to those you love too.

Unearned

*"You are the light of the world. A city
that is set on a hill cannot be hidden."*
Matthew 5:14 NKJV

Imagine if God required us to earn our own
salvation, as many religions or misunderstandings
of Christianity imply. Earning our place in
heaven would be a weighty thing. When we
woke each morning, our minds would fill with
ways we could ensure our acceptance with God.
We'd probably start with a laundry list of things
to do in order to ensure our places in heaven.
Whenever we had free time, we'd be trying to
slip in a few good deeds.

But when those well-meant good deeds
went awry, would we chalk them up to a sin-
filled world or berate ourselves for having done
wrong when we planned on doing right? How
would we escape from the world's tendency to

make even good things fall apart?

The harder we tried, the more we'd focus on ourselves, our failings, and our need to do better. Instead of reaching out to others because God loved them, we'd try to touch them to improve our own heavenly lot. Selfishness would impede all we did.

That's why God doesn't expect us to earn our way into heaven. He settled that issue when He gave us the gift of salvation and freed us to become His light in the world, reflecting the light of His Son, who came to illuminate our lives with knowledge of Him.

Free of the need to secure a place in eternity, we devote ourselves to spreading His light, selflessly sharing the way to the Father whose gift means all to us. Set high above the earn-your-way-into-heaven crowd, we shine brightly and light the path to eternal security in Jesus.

Either/Or

The way of the LORD is strength for the upright, but destruction will come to the workers of iniquity.

PROVERBS 10:29 NKJV

Scripture, especially Proverbs, has a lot of these either/or statements, which basically say you can love God and have this blessing, or you can avoid, ignore, and even hate Him and receive this bad thing.

God offers plenty of blessings to those who love Him. He showers us with good things because He is a good God who wants to share much with us and give us joy. But those who refuse Him receive quite another response from God. They would misuse the strength (or other gifts) He offers. Instead of doing right in the world, they'd make a mess of it. So God withholds good from them and seeks to limit their ability to do harm.

Some may complain that God picks on unbelievers. Why, they may wonder, should they receive destruction instead of at least moderately nice things? Read Matthew 5:45, which points out that God allows some good things to happen to both the just and the unjust person. No one is completely cut off from pleasant things, but God will not give His enemies an unfair advantage or allow them complete control of His loved ones.

Have no doubt about it, this is a war, albeit a spiritual one. Though the last battle may be long off, God takes the conflict seriously. Destruction for those who hate Him is the ultimate end.

But strength, given to believers, allows them to fight on when the enemy seems strong. Blessings are the reinforcements that enable us to go on when the battle becomes hard.

God always gives the right things to the right people—those who trust in Him.

Keeping the Word

"Most assuredly, I say to you, if anyone keeps My word he shall never see death."

JOHN 8:51 NKJV

When Jesus spoke these words, the Jews thought He was mad. The very idea that He was greater than Abraham offended these outwardly faithful Jews. They didn't like the idea that Jesus claimed that much authority.

But these words are obviously a challenge to anyone. They fly in the face of the "practical" world we live in. We don't think Jesus lost His mind, but do we have a hard time believing that eternal life is truly ours? Are we tempted to believe in things that aren't contained in His Word? Do we struggle to believe that the way He laid out for belief in God is really the way—the only way?

Jesus doesn't simply say that those who

believe in His Word shall never see death. Many people can give some mental assent to His teachings, though their hearts haven't been converted. Others have walked the aisle but failed to follow through. Jesus doesn't want people who have followed the "right" formulas. He wants those whose hearts, minds, and spirits are engaged with Him and willing to act on His words.

Those who do that receive a great promise— eternal life, uncounted ages in which to draw even nearer to the One whose Word meant so much in the hours, days, and years of earthly life. Keeping His Word may cost something today, but this world's price will never compare with unending benefits in an eternity of salvation. So when we struggle to keep our faith on track, trust fully in all Jesus said, and live consistently with the scriptures, let's remind ourselves where we're heading: heaven is our real home.

Generous Giver

"Ask, and it will be given to you;
seek, and you will find; knock,
and it will be opened to you."
MATTHEW 7:7 NKJV

Have you ever had anyone offer to give as generously to you as Jesus? If so, did that human follow through on every promise with all you wanted or needed? Not really. No one can give the way Jesus can. People don't have His assets, and even if they did, they can't reach all the hurting places of the heart or give perfect guidance. Jesus not only wants to give, but He gives all we need.

Our huge, aching void, a collection of unmet needs presents a problem to us, or any human. But to Jesus, they are an opportunity to fill us with His love. Or where we cannot forgive, He can empty those closets filled with fear and doubt and replace them with overflowing compassion.

But He doesn't promise to give all we want in a moment. The Christian walk is one of asking, seeking, and knocking. No spoiled children enter heaven, untried and replete with too many good things. God wants us to value the gifts He gives, and anything received too easily is also easily despised. Though He gives wholeheartedly and offers only the best, Jesus will have nothing unappreciated.

When we look back at our lives, will we view a life of thanks for gifts God sent quickly, barely in time, or incredibly slowly, in our opinion? Whether we merely asked, sought, or knocked incessantly, at the end of our lives we'll certainly realize that everything came just in time—God's time. And our praises will ring through all the earth.

Filled Spirit

"Blessed are the poor in spirit,
for theirs is the kingdom of heaven."
MATTHEW 5:3 NKJV

These words describe someone with a character just the opposite of the scribes and Pharisees—respected Jews who would soon become Jesus' main enemies. Though these leaders talked a lot about God, made every effort to look good, and probably had excellent reputations, Jesus described them as "whitewashed tombs" (Matthew 23:27). They may have looked good on the outside, but inside they were disgusting.

Maybe you've met some folks who thought they had a great spiritual life, were proud of their place in the community, and talked a good line about their faith; yet they never cracked open a Bible, and they lived according to their own rules, not God's. Full of their own spiritual importance, they may not have listened when you tried to tell them about real faith.

These so-called spiritually full people head toward destruction at Mach speed, though they don't recognize it. They can't hear Jesus calling them to recognize their own emptiness, instead, and fly to Him for filling.

Only those who know their own inadequacy, when it comes to pleasing God, are ready to be truly full. Instead of clinging to ideas that cannot save or trying to earn their way into heaven, they recognize that all they can offer cannot make them ready for eternity. God must drain them of their own "spiritual" ideas, values, and desires first.

Those who recognize that truth and turn to Jesus are filled with His Spirit and given a new life. Eventually they inherit heaven with Him. But from that first breath of new life, heaven lies within their hearts, and God's filling has begun.

Blessed Mercy

"Blessed are the merciful,
for they shall obtain mercy."
MATTHEW 5:7 NKJV

Give mercy, and you will receive it—that's often true in our world, and it's even more true in eternal terms.

As Christians, we have received God's great mercy. We cannot complain no one offered us compassion, because He gave us so much in one large package marked "salvation." All our sins are behind His back, never to be brought to our attention again. Yet His mercy didn't end there. Daily He renews His gifts as we live for Him. As we wake each morning and go to sleep every night, we can thank Him for His watchful care and ask His forgiveness all over again for the wrongs of the day.

Should we hold on to our mercy and not

pass it on to any we come in contact with each day, we betray God's work. He didn't offer us forgiveness for our sins so that we could hold a grudge against another or demand the final payment for every sin against us. Acting that way ruins our Christian testimony. Satan is the one who demands full payment for every wrong, not God. The Savior offers the blessing of forgiveness based on His life's sacrifice.

But when we offer mercy to others, not only does God approve, people often recognize the good we've done and are more likely to give us a break too. The forgiven offender is likely to be less critical of us when we make mistakes. The one we've helped is usually willing to help us out when we're in a pinch.

This ebb and flow of mercy is just what God had in mind. Mercy, passed around the world by kindhearted Christians, changes a lot of attitudes and hearts.

Looking Ahead

For our present troubles are small and won't last very long. Yet they produce for us a glory that vastly outweighs them and will last forever!

2 CORINTHIANS 4:17 NLT

Have you ever watched a reality TV show where contestants went through all kinds of awful stunts in order to win large amounts of money? Why would anyone do such a thing? Because the promise of the money lured them so strongly that they were willing to do almost anything to get it.

Greed may be a powerful motivator, but it isn't a perfect one. As those shows prove, eventually most people draw a line at something. It's not worth it to put life and health at risk for a huge chunk of change. But you can get most people to do a certain number of distasteful things for a big benefit.

Christians know what it means to suffer for a while to get something even better. But we have a finer motivation than money. Today we go through some troubles—we decide not to take a job that wouldn't please Jesus or we receive mocking from others because we tell of our faith. Some believers even die for their faithful testimony. Why do we put up with such things? Because we look forward to something much better than a big check—our eyes focus on eternity with Jesus.

Yet even those who give up their earthly lives discover that compared to eternity, it was only a small trouble. What could compare to spending "glory that vastly outweighs" with the Savior?

Standing in Strength

*Strength and honor are her clothing;
she shall rejoice in time to come.*
PROVERBS 31:25 NKJV

In a day when dishonesty is often almost taken as a matter of course, a woman whose strength of character demands honesty can stand out in a crowd. Sometimes it's the kind of standing out she'd prefer not to have when her strength leads to uncomfortable situations. A worker who refuses to lie for her boss or to a client or a politician who stands firm on her promises may get some grief and even experience some losses. But no matter how hard it seems, clothing herself in strength and honesty is still the right thing to do. If she stands firm, scripture promises, she'll be glad of it in the end.

Doing right doesn't always make life easy. Many who go with the flow don't appreciate being confronted with their own expendable morals. When an honorable person stands firm against them, they'll attack with all they have and may even try to dislodge the honest one. Right actions can cause Christians to feel intense heat from others.

But that doesn't mean their stance is wrong. There are things worth standing firm for, even if they have a price. Sometimes that price, painful as it may seem, is just what brings the blessing.

No matter how intensely people may attack the strong and honorable woman, He who holds on to her future never will. God may not remove the trouble immediately, but He will eventually bring the blessing; and when that happens, her trials will be entirely worth it.

Are you clothed in strength and honor? Have you begun to pay the price of that faithfulness? Stand firm. In a while, you'll be rejoicing.

River of Love

He changes rivers into deserts, and springs
of water into dry, thirsty land. . . . But he
also turns deserts into pools of water,
the dry land into springs of water.
PSALM 107:33, 35 NLT

Dry to wet or wet to dry, God changes the world at His will, ruling over it in ways we often don't understand. Though scientists spend time in labs or the environment seeking to understand creation, we lag distantly behind the Lord who commands it. Much in His incredibly complex world eludes our understanding.

But deserts and rivers aren't the only things God rules. Though we may question or rebel against this truth, God also rules our lives. Even the most wicked of us cannot go further than God allows, and even the best of us has only so many years to do good works.

What's true of creation is true of us: we too are incredibly complex. Our hearts may hurt for years over a series of wrongs; as they work deep into our souls, they work on our spirits and thoughts in convoluted ways. We may not even understand why we hurt, yet we see the results in our lives.

But just as God perfectly understands our world, He sees into our hurt hearts and spirits. And He can alter a river of hate or doubt into springs of faith and trust. Though that heart change may not happen overnight, with faith and determination to follow God's Word, we can see amazing changes.

As God's healing water seeps into our lives, the trickle touches our souls and change becomes possible. But as we open ourselves to His will and way, the trickle springs up, becomes a stream, a pool, then a river of love.

And all of it started in God's hand.

Planning Mode

You see me when I travel and when I rest at home. You know everything I do.
PSALM 139:3 NLT

Are you the kind of person who likes to plan out your life to the last minute? Or are you so go-with-the-flow that you rarely look ahead more than a short time? No matter what your style, you need one path charted through life. When you walk with God, whether you're a down-to-the-minute planner or a let's-see sort, a plan is always at work in your life. He goes before you to plot the most successful course, show you the way, and make sure you reach your destination.

Most human plans plot a fast and furious course to get to the goal in the shortest amount of time. But God's itinerary is different. He creates rest stops for the weary soul. No person can go on forever without a break. No one can go that directly to a serious objective and not pay the price.

When we make our plans, we need to take God's goals into account. A strategy that follows His laws and includes spiritual aims heads us in the right direction, but one that takes no account for His designs lands us on a path leading to destruction—or at least disappointment.

Have you wondered why a plan didn't work as you expected? Did you make it with God's will as well as your own in mind? Are you trusting Him to lead you in the right way? Or are you fighting Him when He has ordained a period of rest? Remind yourself that yours is not the final plan—His is. Since He knows the final goal, He'll always send you in the right direction.

Always Blessed

In the day of prosperity be joyful, but in the day of adversity consider: surely God has appointed the one as well as the other, so that man can find out nothing that will come after him.

ECCLESIASTES 7:14 NKJV

Sometimes our souls don't feel particularly satisfied. If we lose a job, wonder how we'll pay the rent, and imagine all kinds of dire results, it's hard to feel very peaceful. Prosperous days seem to lie behind us, and we can't look into the future and tell how long we'll be in this situation.

God doesn't allow us to look into the future. That's a good thing, because if we knew the future, we wouldn't need to trust God. One of His best methods of developing our spiritual lives would no longer exist, and we'd enter heaven as weak, spineless beings, not the strong ones He wants to create.

But just as God ordained good things in our prosperous times, He brings good even from our most challenging moments. Unemployment may provide a time for spiritual deepening in many ways, as we cling more firmly to Him and know that all we receive comes directly from His hand. When our days are not filled with work at an office or shop, some temporary ministry may appear.

But whether we are joyful or sad, God still remains faithful. He provides our needs, even if we don't get the lavish things we'd prefer. And He always provides generous spiritual blessings for those who trust in Him. Like Paul, who experienced prosperity and want, we can do all things when we abide in Him (Philippians 4:12–13).

No matter what your circumstances, you can always cling to Jesus—and be blessed.

Church Service

Looking unto Jesus the author and finisher of our faith; who for the joy that was set before him endured the cross, despising the shame, and is set down at the right hand of the throne of God.

HEBREWS 12:2 KJV

What makes a church really successful? I'm not talking about numbers, converts, or depth of programs for different ages but the kind of church that really gets at the heart of faith.

Different people may answer that question various ways. And many of their responses may have validity. But I submit that the one that is successful in Jesus' eyes is the church that looks intently to Him, recognizing the importance of His sacrifice and the need of all to come to Him.

Many congregations claim to be Christian, but how many are seeking Jesus' face? How many understand the critical importance of Jesus and His sacrifice so that we may have eternal life? Some Christians will be stunned that the questions even need to be asked. They've grown up in strong churches and heard the Gospel all their lives. But many who spend lots of years in "church" have never heard the Gospel or gotten its message that only through Jesus can anyone come to God.

A church isn't successful because it sends out missionaries, addresses social issues, or claims to believe in the scriptures. Those are all part of the testimony of the church, but none is the main focus. The only real focus of faith is Jesus, and when we glorify Him, draw close to Him, and recognize our emptiness without Him, we are the real church—the one He rejoiced to serve with His life.

Whom—or what—are you serving today?

Why?

What is man, that thou art mindful of him?
and the son of man, that thou visitest him?
PSALM 8:4 KJV

This is one of those keep-you-up-at-night or make-you-zany questions that looms large in scripture. If we're honest and we look at our omnipotent, perfect Lord, we wonder why He should be mindful of us. It's not as if He somehow needs us the way we require Him. God could do fine, thank you, without our small, confused lives as interferences.

Why God chose to love such unlovely beings is one of scripture's most awesome mysteries. Something inside the Merciful One compelled Him to a series of acts we humans would instantly recoil from. Suffering was not too high a price for Jesus, when the alternative was to leave us languishing in outer darkness for eternity. To draw people to Himself, Jesus willingly paid a huge personal price.

As confused as the psalmist may have felt about God's decision to take on such a costly and seemingly personally unbeneficial love, human ability to apprehend this truth has never increased. We continue the quest to understand God's grace. Thousands of years haven't answered the question, and it could be pondered by humanity for thousands more, without turning up a satisfying clue. The revelation exists in God Himself, His own immense, gracious person, whom we struggle to understand.

On earth, we may never comprehend God's desire or plan, but through the ages, all Christians have joined in worship and praise of One who gives so willingly and generously. While we may never nail down God's motives, we can certainly rejoice in their results, as we experience overwhelming evidence of the Savior's love. Even without an answer, we love Him in return.

Goodness and Mercy

Surely goodness and mercy shall follow me
all the days of my life: and I will dwell
in the house of the LORD for ever.

PSALM 23:6 KJV

God's goodness and mercy come in many
packages and many sizes, but they follow us
each day of our existence. Whether we've passed
through many hard times or just a few, no day
given to any believer following Jesus lacks these
two blessings.

If you have faced many trials on earth, one
day, when you reach heaven, you'll understand
that God saved the best for last—in eternity,
you'll discover He was simply giving you more
honor and blessing in heaven. If yours was a
smoother life, you will not be disappointed with
your heavenly reward if you remained faithful
to the Savior, using your life to help those in

need. God gives us different lives and blessings, designed just for us.

Those blessings provide goodness and mercy on earth and continued joy in heaven. There's no dissonance between our song here on earth and the one that will praise Jesus eternally. Anyone who serves Jesus with energy and love will come to eternity satisfied with His faithfulness. As we forever dwell in the house of the Lord whom we have served, we'll continue to experience His goodness in the real life of heaven—life that is not bombarded by sin or death.

If you love Jesus, goodness and mercy are on your trail today. Just make sure you're on the right track—the one He walked down before you.

Scripture Index

Genesis
18:14 66

Deuteronomy
4:2 72
12:7 84

Joshua
1:8 132

Ruth
1:20 98

2 Samuel
22:51 63

Job
42:12 146

Psalms
1:1, 3 36
8:4 186
18:19 . . . . 92, 100
18:33 62
21:6 10
23:4 . . . . 62, 63
23:6 188
30:5 130
46:1 24
63:3 12
65:5 40
90:14 8
91:16 80
107:33, 35 178
119:103 106
122:1 122
139:3 180
145:3 64
145:16 78
147:8 94

Proverbs
3:12 102
10:29 164
11:25 124
15:29 60
16:24 104
25:17 74
31:25 176

Ecclesiastes
3:11 90
3:12–13 82
7:14 182
12:1 58

Isaiah
1:18 156
12:5 54
29:5 140
33:2 68
40:11 116
41:8–9 56
55:8 14

Lamentations
3:22–23 158
3:31–33 160

Jonah
3:1–2 42
3:8 44

Malachi
3:6 134

Matthew
5:3 170
5:7 172
5:9 128
5:14 162

6:20 118
6:20–21 5
7:7 168
7:11 50
11:28 114
23:27 170

LUKE
12:19 83
17:16 126

JOHN
3:16 86
8:51 166
10:10 46
15:11 112
16:24 48

ACTS
6:8–9 110

ROMANS
13:10 22

1 CORINTHIANS
1:3 30
1:4 28
2:9 70
13:4 76

2 CORINTHIANS
4:17 174

GALATIANS
4:6 136

EPHESIANS
2:4, 6 138

PHILIPPIANS
2:11 108
4:6 152
4:7 154
4:13 150

COLOSSIANS
1:10 26
3:12 18–19
3:15 18
3:19 20

1 THESSALONIANS
5:23 38

2 THESSALONIANS
3:3 142

1 TIMOTHY
4:4 52

2 TIMOTHY
3:16–17 144

TITUS
2:13 148

HEBREWS
10:35 32
12:2 184

JAMES
1:17 16

2 PETER
3:9 34

1 JOHN
2:5–6 88

2 JOHN
9 96

JUDE
2 120

About the Author

Pamela McQuade works as a freelance writer and editor in a suburb of New York City. She and her husband have two basset hounds and a cat and have recently taken up fly-fishing together. In her spare time, Pamela enjoys reading mystery novels, knitting, quilting, and other stitching crafts.